WHY?!

Martin Suiter

WHY?!

Experience, contacts and a creative mind
can not be replaced at all.

Bibliografische Information der Deutschen Nationalbibliothek:
Die Deutsche Nationalbibliothek verzeichnet diese Publikation in der Deutschen Nationalbibliografie; detaillierte bibliografische Daten sind im Internet über http://dnb.dnb.de abrufbar.

© 2014 Martin Suiter, MARTIN SUITER - Consultancy

Cover photo: Kunsthaus Bregenz - Photo © Hélène Binet

Herstellung und Verlag: BoD – Books on Demand, Norderstedt
ISBN: 978-3-7322-7827-5

Content

Credits

It was worthwhile it to spend hours and hours to get this book done, and is a grateful way to thank all the people I met throughout my work over the last 20+ years. All these inspirational and open minded persons I met are the source of my creativity.

Introduction

Dear reader,

writing a book about daily work? You may ask why? Daily new experiences with people and projects reach me, people with diverse backgrounds and challenges. Therefore I would like to share my experiences and results in this book: cases and conclusions from different branches can be found and core aligned to other business fields and markets. The book is a summary of our blog articles from September 2011 to October 2013.

Since 1990, I am in the communications and marketing field and in these years I have seen with my agency many business segments. Large and small. companies, trade companies, destinations, federations and associations have asked me prior to a consultant work: what is the ultimate key to success?

Having looked at the market for years, I found there were many important marketing strategies, whereby the initiators have prevailed for a long time over their competitors. But what does long-term mean in this context? Do you have to constantly re-invent the wheel? I say clearly - NO. Attention is a key element that I use daily, in order to have the right answers to the many varying requirements. In order to develop successful business and communication strategies, the importance is to emphasise the two principles of neuromarketing research:

Without emotions no decision process is possible!

and

Only positive connotations that are associated with a brand make it successful.

Introduction

Repeatedly, emotions play the biggest role in strategies. But how can we evaluate and validate emotions? This is the reason why I am constantly searching for a new, defined approach to give our customers something tangible. The most important point I have learned is that one has to first develop a product and create a brand that has a value in itself. Consequentially a desire / demand will be awakened.

The challenge of a successful project is my motivation and driving factor, no matter whether it is a new or repetitive project. To see the strengthening of a brand and increasing profits for my clients gives me an enormous satisfaction, it goes without saying, the financial aspect should not be ignored ☺

Enjoy my thoughts and ideas. Have I provoked some food for thoughts? Looking forward to receive a call or a mail from you.

Personal regards,

Martin Suiter

MARTIN SUITER – Consultancy
Mail: mail@martinsuiter.com
Internet: www.martinsuiter.com

Marketing

It is an incredibly broad field where there are so many ideas and people cavort who neither have completed specialized studies, nor have a profound knowledge in marketing. Nevertheless, so much intensity has been caused by a very strong identification with the product or the brand that has led to worldwide success. Apple, Google and Facebook are just a few of the best possible examples, plus there is a plethora of wonderful SMEs that have had similar success in their fields.

However, and this is what should never be forgotten, these are not normal cases, but rather the exceptions. Usually, there needs to be very solid work done and a lot of market knowledge is required. Only a comprehensive knowledge of their own and foreign markets guarantees the requirement to bring a product or brand to the market's attention. Requirement? Yes, because I am convinced that this never works without passion. My clients can only be successful if both sides – agency and client – have the internalization of the target in common and work and live with the idea that their goal is worthwhile and achievable. Innovation is a fundamental factor. An innovation may be an utopia because innovation means having an idea which is constantly present in the mind, even if the idea does not seem to be directly implemented. Because the creative spirit is always "open", it recognizes immediately if there is an opportunity, it is the right time or if there is a market for this innovation. Louis Pasteur: "In the fields of observation chance favors only the prepared mind."

Networking – How to

Martin Suiter at IMEX 2013 Frankfurt © Daniela Leonhard

Networking is one of the most important things in business. The following definition proves the point: to socialize for professional or personal gain (www.thesaurus.com: Networking). Impressive: the different kinds of descriptions and terms for this activity – every language has a couple of words for it, which shows its importance. Decisions in (sport-) politics for example, wouldn't be possible without networking: building a circle of followers who are willing to vote for or help you with your concerns in order to give them something they want – the high art of networking!

Time is a big issue. To create relationships takes a lot of time. Trust needs a strong fundament. At the centre of trust you need to prove that people can rely on you. To be a good networker you need to be able to see into the future and to know who you could possibly activate within your network to start a new project.

Instead of emailing or texting use your telephone to get in contact directly. This will shorten things and in the discussion process you can exchange arguments or even find more points that need to be considered, more easily. The modern technique gives you perfect support with Google hangouts or face time so you even can see each other.

But nothing will be able to replace a face to face "meet & greet." For example, exhibitions are the perfect places to be able to build relationships and identify who can help you, who you can trust and who might be important in the future. Do not miss a chance, you never know which business card might be a door opener to someone you did not think about before. Also, exhibitions, workshops, social evenings, etc. are multisensual. Shaking hands, studying behaviour, seeing reactions on both sides – your friends – and your enemies (competitors) – cannot be replaced by any "smart" technology.

Here are some tips for successful networking:

- Quality, not quantity: A network is only as valuable as its members.
- Keep going: If a contact is made, it should be acted upon. Connections must be maintained!
- Take your time to build a network
- Seek contact and be honest
- You need to prove first that it will be good working with you and that others will gain something
- Never cheat
- Use your network only for real concerns

Go East: Is China ready / are we ready?

Palace in Kyoto © Fotolia

When we talk about China we are mostly confronted with preconceptions and expectations on how Chinese customers, clients, business partners are going to behave. But how much of this is true? What is important to know about our Chinese partners? And what expectations do they have in return?

As always when you try to approach a market you must first listen. The Chinese have made massive developments within the last 10 years. What seemed impossible years ago, and where you only found tightly closed doors, might not be the case today and there might be a chance. Thousands of Chinese have studied since then in Europe or America; they have learned our way of life and have become more open to the "western style" without abandoning their roots. But these people are aware of the possibilities. Opening the markets has brought an enormous growth in the middle classes. More money is available but how to spend it? Very rapidly the basic needs have been covered. As in all social communities people look for classification. Other than the Japanese who look for "Bling", Chinese shoppers want long-lasting brands that are hard to get in China and of high quality but no public fuss. This is a perfect reason to shop in Germany, the home of some major quality brands like BMW, Mercedes-Benz, Hugo Boss, Siemens, and many others. Furthermore Germany (like Austria and Switzerland) has a very good infrastructure and is safe and well organised. But there are definitely some changes to be made so that Chinese tourists (shoppers) will be satisfied after their trip to D,A,CH. One reason could be that because of their one-child policy they want to be pampered and most of them do not understand why the shops are not closed to other customers when they are there. Second reason is that the language is certainly an issue that needs to be dealt with along with differences in diet. On the other hand, brands react to shopping "needs" – Gucci e.g. is only selling two bags to one person at a time, so the market does not overflow. Frankfurt sold 180.000 overnight stays in 2012, an increase of 22% compared to 2011. Per stay in Europe they spend € 907,-. But a big issue is that Chinese credit cards (Unionpay) are not accepted in Europe so shops need to buy separate card readers.[1]

Going to China and doing business is also a challenge. Apart from the customs rules on all goods, language is a big issue and it seems like the Chinese are hiding their feelings. You would need a body language translator to be able to "see" what is expected of you, what they will agree to and if they are reliable. (You can find certain behaviour rules on the Internet)

What is possible, if the Chinese want to achieve something, is the fact that Peking says it wants to develop hundred new exhibition & conference centres and they built them within 5 years. Regarding golf, they have the intention to build 2.700 courses within the next 2 years (until 2015) and to "grow" 20 Mio. Golfers before 2020. Is that realistic? We can not know, but experience shows that we must not think from our prospective, but try to understand that with 1.4 Billion people in the country, things are sometimes easier.

I suggest going there to learn and to see what your chances are in this new challenging market.

---

[1] Source: FAZ 25-08-13 Article Hendrik Ankenbrand/Maximilian Kalkhof

Interview with the Neuromarketing expert
Dr. Hans-Georg Häusel

© Dr. Hans-Georg Häusel

In March 2012, I was able to interview psychologist and expert on Neuromarketing Dr. Hans-Georg Häusel. In the marketing brain science and its transfer on questions of consumer behaviour, marketing and brand management - Häusel is one of the worldwide leading experts in these fields. Because of his fascinating and innovative approach he is in great demand as a keynote speaker at national as well as international events.

MARTIN SUITER – Consultancy: On a watch with 24 hours how far is the current state of research in the Neuromarketing field?
Hans-Georg Häusel: That is a difficult question, because a watch ends at the 24th hour. In science we do not know what we are still able to learn. Despite that, I would say we have managed 30% – so it is at 08:00 o'clock.

MARTIN SUITER – Consultancy: How is it possible to "calculate" the influence of the social environment on purchase behaviour?

Hans-Georg Häusel: Our buying patterns are influenced by many factors, like ...

a) Our emotional personal structure (Limbic® Types)

b) Culture (people from Asia have different preferences than people from Western Europe)

c) Social milieu (a female relative of a board member of a market listed company develops different consumption patterns than a female relative of an unemployed couple)

d) Individual learning experiences

e) Actual emotion / a given situation

All these factors need to be considered, no factor is relevant on its own.

MARTIN SUITER – Consultancy: Will mobile micro payments change our buying patterns?

Hans-Georg Häusel: Yes, exactly like our spending increases when we use credit cards instead of cash, because the painful parting with real money is not experienced. Micro payment will ease this – our compulsion to buy will increase moderately.

Hans-Georg Häusel is the head of the group Nymphenburg and author of the tree books "Think Limbic" (Haufe 2001), "Brain View" (Haufe 2004), "Emotional Boosting" (Haufe 2009) and editor of "Neuromarketing" (Haufe 2007). His consultancy background: Brand strategy, Neuromarketing, basic psychological and neurobiological research of consumer behaviour.

Neuromarketing – get inside the emotions

Neuromarketing Congress 2012 at the BMW World in Munich: Prof. Häusel, www.nymphenburg.de and the excellent line up of experts in the field of customer emotions gave an update of the latest brain studies of consumer behaviour. The Lymbic® Mind Map, developed by Prof. Häusel, is a model where different consumer motivation and decision processes can be split and seen on a scientific basis and used for marketing and product development.

Message I

Gut decisions – "the heart has its reasons, which the mind does not know" – Blaise Pascal. That was the statement of Prof. Gigerenzer a worldwide respected Professor whose topic is heuristic. A heuristic person makes decisions with very little time and limited knowledge. He is able to fade out negligibilities and to concentrate on the essentials. He decides within 3 seconds what to do and how to react. This means, if you want to make good decisions you need to rely on your gut instincts. Intuition is a "sensed" knowledge and we are able to experience it because we do have an evolved brain. But remember that the reason we buy is always influenced by our social environment.

Message II

Ap Dijksterhuis is a Dutch scientist whose conclusions are: we seek security first, even when risk taking might give us a better chance to survive. Test your behaviour yourself with the Implicant Association Test from Harvard University and you will find out how your unconsciousness rules your consciousness. It is because that unconsciousness is so strong we need to change our beliefs; to change behaviour to achieve new megatrends in marketing. However, this is a long process.

Message III

Prof. Henseler, Creative Managing Director of Sensory-Minds, a design studio for innovative technologies and new media has reported his findings. "Call to action" needs usability and this is only possible when you give consumers an intuitive way of operating (approach). Furthermore, consumer decisions are made on content relevance. Emotions prepare decisions – it is an automated process, because emotions are embodied and not cerebral.

Summary

"It's all about people and changing their minds." Steve Jobs

Neuromarketing Congress 2013, Part I:
Age Marketing

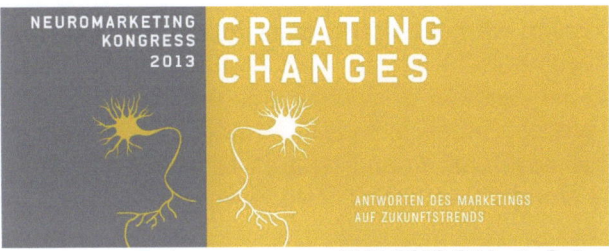

NMK 2013 © Martin Suiter

Munich, BMW Welt, April 25th, 2013: the 6th Neuromarketing Congress was organised by Haufe Verlag and Gruppe Nymphenburg. The sold out congress was as informative and enlightening as in past years. Not only because the issue of the congress "Creating Changes – Answers from the Marketing to the Trends of the Future" is almost related to our company slogan "Creating Business" but because of a lot of useful information. Herewith we want to share a couple of interesting aspects gathered from the lectures.

First of all: Age Marketing with aspects from Prof. Dr. Lutz Jäncke (Neuropsychology, University of Zurich) and Dr. Gundolf Mayer Hentschel (CEO Meyer-Hentschel Institut).

What are the best methods to prevent the process of brain ageing? According to Prof. Dr. Jäncke it is constant mental and physical activity and social contact. Both medical "miracle cures" and nutrition play only a minor role in preventing brain ageing.
In this context, positive changes in brain function can be measured after only 5 hours of "brain strain". So, use it or lose it!

"Politeness in Marketing" – this is the key in Age Marketing according to Dr. Gundolf Mayer Hentschel. The requirements are: intelligent, quiet and user-friendly packaging, well-designed products and businesses that have been designed for clients of all ages and can withstand the higher demands and the differentiated judgement of this target group. With simple modifications to the products tremendous effects can be achieved with older customers – without using the message "you're old"!

The social function of shopping is especially important in older groups. These include: the quality of human contact with the customer. Friendliness is more important than expertise along with a sufficient degree of patience.

MPV (My Personal View): I'm always annoyed that the inscriptions in the hotel shower for shower gel, shampoo, conditioner, etc. are written so small that I can barely decipher them. It would be quite simple to solve this in an age-friendly way.

Neuromarketing Congress 2013, Part II: Gender Marketing

NMK 2013 © Martin Suiter

Part II of our review on the Neuromarketing Congress 2013 (April 25th, BMW Welt in Munich), this time with aspects on Gender Marketing.

"Different by nature? Gender differences from the perspective of psychology" by Prof. Dr. Norbert Bischof Köhler:

From the age of two years, the sexes separate and emerge in different ways. Culture is capable of change, but human nature remains constant. Therefore, we also learn things that do not comply with our natural instincts as a man or a woman. But if it complies with these dispositions, then it is easier and more fun to learn things. Women and men will always act differently and have varying approaches.

"The customer is female" by Diana Jaffé:

Why this title? Because 90% of all everyday consumption decisions are made by women (GFK 2004). But in many marketing heads the main theme is still "shrink it and pink it" to dispose products to women – clearly this thinking is not based on the self-reflection of women at all.

What causes the differences between men and women? First of all, biology (physique, the 5 senses, metabolic processes, brain structure, hormonal influences), and of course sociology and psychology. Women choose to buy a product and then they use a long list of criteria to choose a specific product of one of the manufacturers.

Do things have a gender? Yes, they do! This is at least, one thing men and women agree on, because both say:

Chainsaw = 97% male – vase = 96% female – Department stores = 84% female.

Neuromarketing Congress 2013, Part III: Trust Marketing & Global Marketing

NMK 2013 © Martin Suiter

Part III of our review on the Neuromarketing Congress 2013 (April 25th, BMW Welt in Munich), this time with aspects on Trust Marketing and Global or Culture Marketing.

Cirk Sören Ott ("Brand trust = Trust marketing" – Gruppe Nymphenburg) and Prof. Dr. René Riedl ("How trust is created in the brain" – Johannes Keppler University Linz, Austria) were the speakers on the session "Trust Marketing".

According to them, scandals can hurt a brand primarily by the enormous loss of customer trust. They showed the audience how trust can be created, what options are available to build customer trust and that it can have serious consequences if this trust is recklessly put at risk. Furthermore, a constant change of perspective is essential to properly assess the purchasing behaviour of customers and then it is possible to use this perspective for brand strategy.

The session "Culture and Global Marketing" was held by Prof. Dr. Ernst Pöppel ("Cultural Neuroscience – things that unite cultures, things that separate them" – Ludwig-Maximilians-University Munich) and Dr. Hanne Seelmann-Holzmann ("Megatrend Asia! Go East – but with the right (marketing) instruments" – Seelmann Consultants).

How can a brand image be built? What is important? Our brain stores its best information in 3-second intervals – whether we zap through TV programmes, read verses in a poem or listen to music.
In Asia, advertising messages are often perceived differently than in Europe. Huge mistakes can be made in the translation of brand name or advertising slogans. The loss of customer trust through these mistakes can take very long for companies to repair.[2]

---

[2] The information of the Neuromarketing Congress gathered by Martin Suiter were compiled and formulated by Daniela Leonhard, Social Media Coordinator MARTIN SUITER – Consultancy.

Fantasy vs. Dreams

BMW i3 © Martin Suiter

What is the difference between fantasy and dreams. First of all, a dream is focused on one issue whereas fantasy needs a lot more space. Fantasy has no borders and gives you freedom in any direction you wish to go. It is so important to use fantasy of the imagination in business to see beyond the horizon and see places nobody has ever set foot on.

But be aware of not losing ground. Fantasy is just the ignition you have to be sure that there is something that can "burn" so to speak. Or to be less philosophical: If you have a "far reaching"" idea there must be people that understand what you are intending to do and people that also believe in this idea before you can use it. Creativity is needed to be able to see the solutions that might give you the fantasy born idea. But without knowledge, all this creativity is useless because you will not be able to convert your idea into something useful for your business.

Often, when I sit in meetings and come up with an idea "men in suits" say: "yes, but …" or "we haven't ever done that". Women in costumes answer: "we better stick to what we have done so far". My simple question is: WHY? I agree, sometimes we need to improve the way we tell people things because we are also capable of using other routes and breaking routines and that is never comfortable. There must be people involved who want to alter things and to achieve new levels. Time is a big issue. You need to be able to estimate the right time and sometimes it is wiser to keep a "fantasy" idea to yourself until the right time comes. Reinhold Messner, the famous mountaineer, has a definition for that: Realutopie – that's for when he has an idea, but the time to develop it hasn't yet come. It is an utopia for now, but in his heart he knows exactly that one day it will become reality.

Summary:
Use fantasy to be able to see things that have not yet materialized. Use time to help you find the right period to go public. Be wise and do not forget ROI.

Prostitute yourself

© Martin Suiter

By receiving a task (PR & Communication, Marketing, ...) for a project where you are the voice of someone or something you need to state very clearly in a contract the duties you have that you are able to solve and that are also within the guidelines of your company.

Your own duties:
There must be an agreement of the exact date from when your company takes over to when the mission ends. Especially in these social media days, where actions and reactions can be monitored, it is crucial to set deadlines. Within these guidelines you can be held responsible. On the other hand, the client must be able to react by himself after your mission has finished. Otherwise complaints, damaging comments etc, ... can affect the company's business dramatically and ugly rumours can be difficult to disprove.

Your capabilities:
Are you aware of what you are able to achieve? The outline in the communication field is hard to define. Do your employees understand your client's mission, your client's needs, and your client's philosophy? Everybody involved has to have 3D knowledge – your customers, their clients and the knowledge of the community (especially in the field of Social Media). Also technically there could be a large amount of expenses, e.g. being online for long periods of time, to have access all the time and everywhere and to up- and download the information needed.

Your guidelines:
At the end, when all parameters are agreed, you need to ask yourself – do I want to be involved in this job? Do you want to be an ambassador? Is it a project that reflects my company the way I want it to? Is the team you are working with capable enough to understand the size of the project and do they understand the industry sector? And if not: are they willing to trust you and let you work in your own way? Do they accept you as a team member? If not – do not "prostitute" yourself.

IMEX 2012: How to push your brand

The Alps © Martin Suiter

@IMEX12 I had the privilege to speak at the Inspiration Centre twice. Here is a brief review on what I had to say to the interested MICE (Meeting, Incentive, Congress, Events) people.

Pictures & words can influence us so much. Why are brochures so badly written or the pictures in them bear no connection to the words or the message? Because marketing agencies do not listen to experts in their field. They do not deal with the subject. Corporates, destinations, and hotel chains just pay and believe that a major or expensive and trusted agency is doing the best/right thing. Wrong – it is always the company that needs to know what they want to come across as deeply authentic and to reach the emotional Touch Points on their Customers Journey. Always remember our emotions are embodied and not cerebral.

Meeting People – become an Optionist

Everyone in the MICE business needs to meet and see each other to gain more information face to face, and to share knowledge and experience the verbal and nonverbal input. This is what exhibitions, congresses, workshops, and seminars are for. No Social Media technology can replace that – yet. We think we are so individual and every customer and client is also as individual, but when it comes to call to action buying is a social decision. The whole social environment influences the business with an individual. That is why we need to understand the system and that is why changing behaviour takes so long.

Summary – become a Futurist

You do not need to invent new things for everything, but you need to know how to surprise and how to involve the right partners – to see reality is one thing but to see the possibilities is something different. Be aware that you need to give more than 100% to achieve something special. Like Steve Jobs said: "there must be a better way". So change your way of thinking and step back from USP and turn to ESP (emotional selling proposition) to touch your clients on their customer journey.

Award – Reward – Return Service

Die drei Zinnen, Suedtirol © Martin Suiter

Nearly every day we see pictures from award ceremonies everywhere and for all kinds of things. Why is that? In past times awards were given for outstanding performance in different categories. The Nobel Prize is an example of why an award should be given – for long term, intense analysis, research in various fields and outstanding achievements. It is an award that is given after results have been proven for a long time period.

It is not comparable to the vast amount of awards given nowadays. The reason why an award is given has no connection to real merit any more. The main reasons for awards today are – a reward for return service for booked advertisement space, for booked floor space at exhibitions, for getting famous people to promote products or to attract the press and to showcase the right pictures.

Do you know any award that is given for real substantial work/merit?

In my opinion, only a few people's-choice-awards reflect the popularity of a product or the effort that has been taken. But even this is subject to very short term and temporary moods. Today we are able to let people follow the process of finding the right person, project, product, service to be awarded. In my mind transparency would help to regain value to any kind of Award.

What do you think makes an award worthwhile?

We will follow up that discussion and hope to find a meaningful solution to stop that Award cheating all over.

Do you know your brand advocates?

© stillkost, Fotolia

Your brand is determined by: What you say / Who you are / What others say about

Some facts show the importance of "What others say" about your brand or company:

- 94% trust word of mouth (Forrester Research)
- 67% of US economy impacted by Word of Mouth (Mc Kinsey & Co)
- 31% of brand advocates have increased spending at their primary retailer (IBM)

Brand advocates were always there but now they have the chance to be heard.

What?
A brand advocate is a customer who has favourable perceptions of a brand, who can help generate brand awareness and can influence potential customers better. An advocate

convinces others to purchase through independent credibility by putting his own reputation on the line. BUT advocates don't want to be bought!

You can distinguish between three different types of consumers:
1. Brand advocates are innovators & early adopters – want to convert others
2. Brand loyalists – express their love for a brand to others
3. Consumers – like the brand but don't engage

Who?
Brand advocates are socially well-connected, express opinions and viewpoints, continually discover new content online & need an audience.

Why?
1. Brand advocates are power sharers
2. Brand advocates are engaged
3. Brand advocates bring an established audience
4. Brand advocates are loyal
5. Brand advocates already love your brand.

How to?
The first step to start communication with your brand advocates is to ask yourself the following questions:
- How important are "influencers" for your business?
- Do you target them?
- On which platforms are they active?
- How will you reward them?
- Can you reinforce their loyalty?

New marketing strategies for Millennials

Millennials © Garry Knight

Did you know that Millennials represent the generation with the strongest purchasing power? After the Baby Boom (those born between 1946 – 1964) and Generation X (born between 1965 and 1980), Millennials (born between 1981 and 2000) are the largest, most powerful and valuable consumers on the market since the Baby Boomers. In fact they are spending about $ 170 billion worldwide per year, which makes them the most interesting target group for marketers around the globe.

There are a couple of distinctive characteristics, which make them different from other generations. Because they grew up using the computer, cell phone and laptop, and not knowing life without the Internet, they adapt fast to innovation. The combination of cultural diversity, technology and an active environment has resulted in the ability to multitask, the need for constant entertainment as well as the lack of a long attention span. But what exactly are the interests of this generation and how can they be reached effectively?

Based on specific patterns, Millennials demand an unique marketing strategy. The global leader in assessing the digital world and digital marketing intelligence comScore Inc. published a new whitepaper about next generation marketing strategies for Millennials. The report is based on more than 40 years of advertising research and tries to answer the following questions:

- Is digital advertising a more effective way to reach Millennials than traditional television advertising?
- Are there unique ways to influence the Millennial generation?
- Do Millennials require a total different advertising strategy than other generations?

It is not surprising that marketers are keenly interested in a better understanding of this group and how to effectively reach them. But it is not only marketers who need to understand the generation Millennials. The change in consumer behaviour has an impact on all economic sectors. So ask yourself this:

Is your crisis really caused by the crises or did you miss the changes in consumer behaviour?

Tourism and Hotels

We all love travelling. Whether, we are only in our own garden, on the balcony, in our home country or in the near and far abroad. The thought of discovering new things always motivates us and makes us leave familiar things and experience the new and different. Covering 100% of its own market is utopian, but 80% is possible when you know the rules of the market and remain true at the same time.

Everything is possible to find on the Internet, but is no substitute for personal experience. Therefore, people will travel further and try to feel good by having holiday experiences in all parts of the world. Now, all the hotels have running hot water, and many have even realized that they need free Wi-Fi. Above all, the most important thing is to take home a positive holiday experience, the feeling of being welcome. Genuine warmth and empathy are irreplaceable.

Tourism meets Industry: Ecological competence becomes competitive advantage

TMI 2013 © Martin Suiter

Seefeld (Tyrol), Oktober 10th, 2013: For the second time the cross-industry, international forum TMI – Tourism meets Industry with a huge number of experts from tourism, industry and economy took place. New approaches in the area of mobility as well as energy management and efficiency of cable railways were discussed. The goal is to accelerate effective developments to sustain the Alps as a "smart region".

Here are some insights from the interesting lectures and workshops of TMI:

Prologue 1: Andreas Reiter (ZTB Zukunftsbüro) – "Innovation in Tourism": The greater question is: how will people consume mobility in the future? The answer is on demand (situational mobility), with respect to nature and with consideration for sustainability. Conclusion: The new "Green Lifestyle" requires strong cooperation between ecology and economy.

Prologue 2: Roland Zegg (grischconsulta) – "Energy management as a marketing tool": This prologue was aimed to raise awareness about energy consumption in alpine tourism. For example, the power consumption of all mountain railways in Switzerland is at the same level as the consumption of the city of Chur with 35,000 inhabitants.

Workshop "Mobility in Tourism": New approaches require a global climate strategy and "first movers". In alpine tourism, for example, there are the marketing networks "Alpine Pearls" (slogan "Naturally gentle holiday"), the model community electric mobility Garmisch-Partenkirchen "e-GAP" and the project called "Südtirol Rad". The visions of "first movers" create emotions, desire, and a sense of community, so that customer demand for sustainability is satisfied.

Forum: "Innovative Thinking": Kathrin Aste (LAAC Architekten ZT GmbH) – "Sustainable Design for alpine Infrastructure": Mountain peaks are landmarks and cannot be destroyed by windmills. So here also, new technology is required. Following natural logic, LAAC found a solution in developing vertical windmills that can be huddled against the rocks so they can hardly be seen from the valley. This is a more efficient way to use the chimney effect that carved mountain gorges have. The so called Alpine Hybrids can be productive both in wintertime and summertime.

"Innovation Projects E-Mobility": Dr. Julian Weber (BMW Group) – BMW is pursuing a new strategy: The drive for innovation is the desire for change from the outside (environment, urbanization, politics, economy, culture, customer ...). The challenge is to combine the brand promise and driving pleasure with the sustainability from the development up to the "scrapping". New motto: Born Electric.

High art of Quality Management

Hotel Metropole Hanoi © Martin Suiter

Quality Management is my favourite subject. It takes a lot of energy to be more service oriented than the rest – the other competitors. In the hotel business especially, it is understood that wherever you "lay your head on the pillow" there is warm water and a TV, sometimes even free Wi-Fi. But what makes me want to come back is "quality oriented" staff that is trained enough to handle things independently and give me the best personal hospitality. This regardless of if I stay one night or 14 nights and if I pay a high rate or a family & friends rate.

Quality also means that as the guest I do not have to worry about things that are the staff's responsibility. For example: at breakfast – there is often a waiter who walks around with a coffee pot as if to ask: "Would you like some coffee?" my answer is "No thanks, I would like to have some fruit tea". The answer will invariably be "Oh, the tea buffet is over there, help yourself" as the waiter points to the far end of the room. Why do they do that? There are other examples:

Waiters who say "Sorry, I only have coffee with me, but I would be delighted to get you your tea, which kind of tea would you prefer?" Which of the two replies would you like to hear? What I really do not understand is when I have stayed in a hotel many times, they have me in the CRM system – "likes a quiet room" – even when the front desk staff is reading that loud and confirming it to me during check-in, I end up in a loud room. After complaining, I then get a quieter room, but why the hell not in the first place! Regarding complaining, I hate to listen to staff who is speaking badly about other staff or sharing private things that I can't overhear. Also, I do not want to see staff smoking outside the hotel, standing around and checking on new arrivals with a raised eyebrow. So, Quality Management means really engaging with your work, well trained staff and really good professional management. After all, the staff reflects a good director.

Quality Management means that you do things ahead of your competitors and give out signals "that it is worth working together". Top German newspapers got together and did a survey on high quality journalism and advertising. The outcome was that if you do your marketing campaign in a high profile and quality newspaper it is much more likely to be successful and stay longer and more deeply in the reader's, your future or actual customer's or client's minds. What impressed me is that they did not complain about the difficult times the print business has but rather, started to find arguments to show and prove that it is worth investing in quality.

What makes your hotel stay memorable

Bregenzer Wald © Martin Suiter

Sometimes just a few words make a difference. This time I will guide you to the beautiful "Bregenzer Wald". It is a destination in Austria east of Lake Constance well renowned but still undiscovered and especially in autumn, a hidden gem. I would like to introduce you to two hotels both with a long tradition in hospitality but with a very different projection.

The "Gasthof Hirschen Schwarzenberg" is mentioned for the first time in 1601 and even Bavarian King Max II. slept here over night. With every step you can "feel" the tradition, smell the history through the well-restored wood panels and enjoy regional but exceptional food and wine. It is a hotel for intellectuals with reading corner. The rooms are stuffed with art and on long winter nights there are readings and special concert nights with classic, jazz, blues and even rock music held. The cold and seemingly hostile world is left outside and inside you feel the warmth of the fireplace with its flickering candles and you feel safe and at home.

The "Hotel Post Bezau" also has a long tradition and is today run by Susanne Kaufmann, (fifth generation). Opened as a post station in 1850 it became a guesthouse and in 1968 it was renovated and extended as a sport hotel. Today Susanne Kaufmann established the style, wellness and culinary island within a wonderful alpine surrounding. Also here the warm chimney and the comfortable bar make the guests feel welcome. For women and men the treatments with Susanne Kaufmann's own biological beauty cosmetics and crème series are located in the basement which is all furnished in white. A full contrast to the autumn red, orange and green colors of the Bregenzer Wald. It is interesting to note that they present themselves as a traditional hotel (Post), as a name branded hotel (Susanne Kaufmann) and as a wellness hotel (Best Wellness Hotels).

The difference between these two hotels – I never get tired of mentioning, no matter what establishment you are in, whether it is 5 star or a farmhouse, whether it is a design or traditional hotel, guesthouse or restaurant – it is all about people and offering a personal service. All year round I spend about 120 nights on the road and sleep in 60- or 70 different hotels. They all have warm and cold water, a bed and food to offer. When I look back, however, I remember the few but very important personal exchanges with the staff (room service, restaurant, reception, spa) that have made my stay special and made me feel like I am now an ambassador for that place and would recommend it to my friends and colleagues. The Hirschen has exceptional staff where you feel that they are more than happy to serve you and make your stay as good as they possibly can. At Susanne Kaufmann's place the staff is well trained but you get the feeling that some of them are "just working" there. Some are wonderful, as you would expect them to be, but some of them are missing the quantum that makes your stay more than enjoyable.

Change from Tradition to the Modern times

Tourism Workshop, University of Innsbruck (Tyrol), May 2013. This is the outcome of the tourism workshop that I conducted with students at the University of Innsbruck. The question was: What service could the 5 star hotel Interalpen offer to manage the change from traditional to modern times?

© Hotel Interalpen

After 45 minutes of consultation each of the 4 groups presented their thoughts, which I summarise here:

Activities:
- There is a famous peace bell near the hotel. Therefore the hotel could organise peace workshops to reflect the peace situation at seminars. At the end there could even be a manifest.
- Culinary picnics using local products guided by the producers. The guests, in addition, would be able to share local knowledge.

Marketing:

- Instead of the overload of emails, why not send the key guests little presents like an Easter egg or a small football for the Champions League final, when it is time for that?
- The students recommended stepping back from guest comment cards or letters on the room or email questionnaires after the stay. They argued that the self-image of such a hotel must be so strong, that there is no need for such a survey. Nevertheless, all employees need to be encouraged to listen strongly to every overheard comment and pass these on to the management.
- Facebook is not the right channel to reach and to communicate with these premium hotel guests. Furthermore, the guests are so different that this channel would only reach a small group.

The best point the students made in my eyes was to create an APP, but an APP that would work for all the hotels that these guests book. In this case for all Leading Hotels of the World. The APP would definitely change the communication between guest and hotel. The key contents need to be:

Before booking:

- All details of the hotel and the actual hotel activities with the possibility of pre-booking (massage, personal trainer)

After booking:

- All travel information (road works, union strikes, (weather forecast, ...). Tips what to wear, special lookout points and directions to the hotel)
- How should the room be prepared (which fruits, which water, mini bar stocking and monitoring, thickness of mattress, time of arrival so the room can be ready, preferred newspaper, favourite dish, or diet sheets, preferred departure time)

During the stay:
- Direct contact to housekeeping, reception, restaurants (with seat plan for booking a table),
- All room lights, music, curtains, TV, etc. should be controllable through the APP
- Tick boxes to get instant messaging / reminder for massage appointment, that the Sunday paper is now available, drink of the day, certain information for women and children etc.
- Around the hotel (restaurants, places to see or things to do, doctors (including interpreters)
- Pool or terrace or garden service (food or drink order through the APP which also contains the special of the day or local specialities)
- Cooking classes of local specialities with local chefs

Mindful thoughts of the hotel:
- Create and cherish partnerships with local producers and local providers. That could even include a self- paying system so all expenses could be billed directly to the room. Agreements that guests can eat at the Chinese restaurant, for example, and this can be used as part of the half board.
- Organize special events at landmarks or museums only for hotel guests (e.g. after closing time)
- Handwritten notes placed in the room (on the mirror, for example, "Bad hair day? Need a hairdresser immediately? Book through our app!")
- Private cars (no Taxi sign on top)
- Bedding not too hard, towels not too soft and not smelling of chlorine
- Laundry basket
- Lettering on the shower gel, shampoo and conditioner must be large enough
- Twist-off cap should be easy to open with wet hands
- Unobtrusive cosmetics

- A calm atmosphere in the entrance hall and around the reception
- High-class handling
- No overload of offers
- Discreet handling of guest's requirements
- Employees must communicate with each other very politely
- Efficient and speedy check out
- Hints for "last scenic view back to the hotel"

After stay:
- Send on lost & found items but with a consolation (chocolate to ease the loss of the missing goods)
- Send hotel postcards "This place misses you"

It was great fun and inspirational to see the engagement and enthusiasm of the students. I'm looking forward to more workshops to come!

Do you have any more information or aspects you want to share with us? Any further comments from you are welcome!

© Hotel Interalpen

Complimentary Wi-Fi – a hotel must-service?

Hotel München Palace © Stephan Kuffler

In spring 2013, we published the "Free-Wi-Fi Hotel List" on the MARTIN SUITER – Consultancy Facebook page. This list shows a collection of 4 or 5 star hotels that provide complimentary Wi-Fi for their guests. Reason for the list: It bothered us that on our business or holiday trips, many of the hotels still do not offer complimentary Wi-Fi. And we want to show alternative hotels that have this service included! – Well, we know that in effect, it is not really free, but it feels better if we automatically get access and do not have to pay for it so obviously.

Two points that hotels ignore by charging for Wi-Fi: First - many men and women on business trips do not have a budget for paying extra and the company won't pay for it, consequently they do not use Wi-Fi, which means hotels are not allowing these people contact with their families!! These travellers will then not use FaceTime or Skype to stay in contact with their loved ones. But 78% say that being away from the family is the most negative aspect of being on business trips. Second - these hotels welcome their guests, but fail to allow them to be able to tell anybody!! By using Facebook, Foursquare etc. they miss the chance to use their guests as prospective ambassadors.

Another point to discuss, apart from Wi-Fi is - breakfast. In German hotels breakfast needs to be named as an extra on the invoice, which means that breakfast is not deductible. However, I found a smart hotel that didn't use breakfast as a term. Instead, they wrote "business package" on the invoice. That makes everybody happy – except, of course, the taxman!

Some critical comments have already reached us, which we'd like to take up and to discuss here.

Jamie Rogers on LinkedIn wrote: "It's never truly complimentary / free. We pay for all amenities one way or the other at hotels. I recently stayed at the Omni in Providence RI and was 'given' free WIFI. Except the WIFI was down the entire time I was there. Great perk!"

Chuck Hicks on LinkedIn: "In this day and age, it should always be provided and free if you are a valued customer and regular user of the brand."

Let's discuss!

Free Wi-Fi in hotels? Results of a constructive discussion

In March 2013, we started a discussion concerning the necessity of complimentary Wi-Fi in hotels. The response to this discussion was tremendous and extremely constructive. More than 65 industry professionals from around the world shared their thoughts on this matter.

What we have learned: Most of the participants think that complimentary Wi-Fi is definitely a must-have service in a hotel and that they wouldn't book a hotel without complimentary Wi-Fi. Even most of the hotel industry professionals said that these days, complimentary Wi-Fi is an essential need and had become an expected commodity.
However, it's important to summarize the results regarding the two different perspectives that crystallized during the discussion: the "guest perspective" and the "hotel perspective". So we've tried to create a pros and cons list with regard to the different point of views.

Some of the participants in this discussion suggested compromises such as:

- Free low bandwidth Wi-Fi, fast Wi-Fi with fee
- Not a must for budget hotels, but certainly a must for 4 stars hotels upwards
- Free Wi-Fi for Loyalty Program Members as a reward (example IHG)

So, what do you think? Complimentary Wi-Fi in hotels: Yes or No? And Why? Find the Pros and Cons in the following.

You have more Pros or Cons? Let us know!

Free-Wi-Fi Pros & Cons: Guest & Hotel Perspective:

	PRO	CON
Guest	- staying in contact with family & friends - checking business mails, facilities nearby the hotel, other business information - business travel: less costs for company	- if it's slow, it's worth than paying for a faster Internet access
Hotel	- marketing tool I: sign in page to gather customer information (email, etc.) - marketing tool II: promote new services, specials etc. on the welcome page - marketing tool III: guests advertise indirect for the hotel by posting that they are there - attract the local business market (for business meetings with F&B) - reduce the overall cabling to the rooms and public areas = huge stock of savings - attracts more business guests - customer service in general - fulfilling guest expectations & increase satisfaction - otherwise disadvantage to other providers in this mobile & connected world	- high costs to provide high bandwidth and accessibility - danger for property's public network security (e.g. illegalities on the net)

Hotel booking – Alternatives to HRS, Booking.com & Co.?

Mount Falcon © Martin Suiter

When booking a hotel room most people visit the websites of HRS, Booking.com or other Internet sites, to inform themselves about the hotel, prices, etc. and read reviews from other guests to decide which hotel might be the best for their requirements. However, the purpose of these website providers is not only to inform but also to bring the user to the point of making a booking through their website. Simple reason, because with every booking on their website, the providers get about 15% commission of the room costs.

For hotels it is a loss of money and, furthermore, less opportunity to get directly in contact with their guests and show them how valuable they are to them. And for hotel guests? What are the advantages of booking your room through HRS and Co.? And wouldn't there be other and many more advantages, even discounts, by not using the big platforms?

So, are there alternatives out there? YES, there are! Apart from booking or reserving directly through the hotel website or by phone (yes, by phone!) here are some alternative ideas:

A smart, but only available in the US, concept is provided by Guestmob. You choose not only a hotel, but a hotel collection, a group of 4 or 8 hotels in the vicinity of your destination. Specify by choosing the star rating that fits best for your budget. Then book your hotel collection and one of the hotels in that collection is guaranteed to accommodate you. Therefore, it is possible to save up to 50% of the Best Available Rate.

Another newly developed platform is Roomkey. Founded by the world's leading hotel brands like HILTON Worldwide, HYATT or Marriott, this searching and booking platform with offers of hotels worldwide, provides lowest rates guaranteed. As a guest, you earn loyalty points with every booking that you can then use for upgrades or special treatments. And: You book the best rooms direct from the hotels.

Following, you'll find more links to interesting hotel booking platforms. If you miss a platform or service, feel free to comment and suggest the missing platform to us.

HotelHub: Over 275.000 hotels for business related travel

HotelClub: Over 74.000 hotels in 141 countries worldwide. Best Price Guaranteed. Members get up to 7% back on every booking.

reise-10.de: No commission to a provider – instead, 10% discount for the guests who book directly at the hotel (in German and hotel offers in Germany only)

Service Design Tourism – do you service?

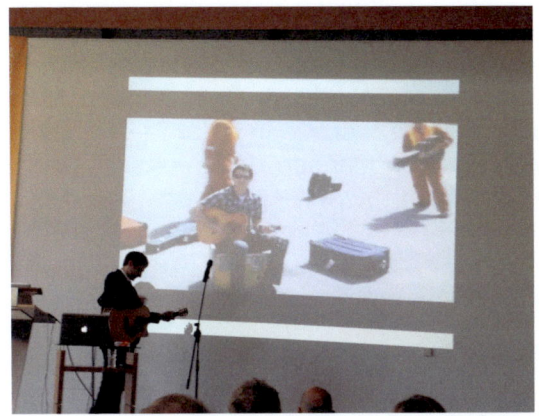

Dave Carroll at SDT2012 © Martin Suiter

My prejudice design is cool, black, square, glass, men in black suits and max. white shirts, Apple, distinction, snobbish, wannabe, etc. But what do these preconceptions have to do with hospitality, warmth, hearty welcomes and service? Frankly, – nothing at all, but Service Design seen as a result of designing the service to suit your guest – gets us closer to the powerful meaning.

One conclusion I made at the SDT2012 was that my fellow colleagues who work in the tourism industry, experience every day that all servants (all who come into contact with the guests) in the industry still misunderstand and misinterpret what a guest feels, expects, and what their idea of service is. Instead of asking "how can I best serve your needs?" they still give the impression of: "I have to offer this or that." Dave Carroll singing live at the SDT2012 inspired them, and made the participants think of what service design means: "United breaks Guitars" – Watch his video on YouTube (www.youtube.com/watch?v=5YGc4zOqozo)!

So let's try and turn the thinking around: service means to fulfil expectations, being authentic, being hearty and being as individual as you possibly can. So the often mentioned "Customer Journey" which starts from the search engines on the computer or smart phone till weeks after the stay must be harmonized with your guest and the "bigger picture" needs to be seen. To achieve this we need to follow the "hospitality road" to success. In order to be able to perform in the best possible manner, design (strict manners) must be implemented in the serving process. The main provider (mostly the hotel) is at the end responsible for the quality of service for the whole trip (booking, transportation, accommodation, third parties, and many more).

So physical Service Design is the base to get service experience.

Corporate Cooperations – originality pays off

Macrahanish © Martin Suiter

Leading-, Best Wellness-, Top-, Family-, Boutique-, Design-Hotels – just to name a few, is a trend that brings special interest groups together. Does that make sense and what do you need to be aware of if you join cooperation like this?

Yes, it does make sense – but you need to calculate very carefully. You should know every single hotel (golf course) and the management that is part of that group, because every single partner will represent your values too. In addition, you must commit to sharing costs of marketing activities such as exhibition stands, brochures, web and social media presence. To me the most important issue is: yes, you are a group but you are a group of individuals. Each and every one within the cooperation still needs to be identifiable by their own character, their own authenticity. That could be a special service, special geographical places, size, facilities, furnishing, etc. – in the end, you are competitors.

The challenge is for you to be you. Show your clients, guests and customers within that special interest group your identity. The most important thing is hospitality – make your guest feel at home even before they arrive. Treat every guest as if they were the first you had ever had. Show them that you really care about everything that matters to them. To be able to do so successfully – listen!! Be a good audience and respond as quickly and transparently as you can. Social Media, therefore, could be of major importance. It is mutual and it shows that you do not hide anything.

Conclusion: use every possible network or cooperation even if it is not from the same industry. Make everyone you have to deal with your ambassador.

HRS, TUI vs. Google

A-ROSA Kitzbühel © Martin Suiter

How are you found in the WWW? More booking platforms, more booking co-operations, more DMOs, ... This friction does not help you to get a unique selling proposition and is possibly more expensive than you think. Have you ever calculated how much money you pay on provisions to diverse booking platforms? Would it not be more effective to invest that amount in your own campaign or be more present at exhibitions to meet your client / guest in person? See fairs like www.cmt-golf.de. Or even hire ambassadors (lobbyists) for your hotel? See websites like www.insiderei.com. Or invest in your own mobile strategy? Google did a study and they predicted that in 2014, more than 35% of the bookings with a value over! € 1.000,- will be done with smart phones.

My Personal View (MPV) is that to be successful in the online market you need to be absolutely reliable, open, and give a true impression that your advertisement and pricing is not hiding any costs or "tricks". With all "fast" information, pictures are more important than ever. "Who controls the pictures, controls the heads" (Bill Gates). A top best practice regarding pictures and emotions is the hotel website of D-Hotel Maris. The ADAC (automobile club) Germany did a survey (2012) with its 16 Mio. (2008) members. 70.6% organized their travel themselves. That means that regular package holidays are not relevant any more (except special interest vacations or excursions on special dates or to exceptional geographical areas).

Conclusion: HRS, TUI and others will struggle to be relevant. Google, with its hotel finder, will fulfil all needs. The main point will be that Google has no friction and because of the mass market the provision will be less than it is today. If so, it will be even more important to show your presence on social media platforms, to interact with your guests and clients, to be open and honest, to get a higher ranking because people talk about you. Rethink what you want to achieve and with what kind of strategy.

Destinationcamp, Hamburg 2012 © Martin Suiter

Everybody – Federation, Association and Industry – does it, but are we in the travel industry shouting loud enough and showing our strength? 2012 during ITB the ministry of economy and innovation revealed numbers on billboards. In Germany alone, there are 2.9 Mio. employees (7% of all wage earners) working in the tourism industry and Germany has 394 million overnight staying guests per year. That is worth 280 billion Euros of total revenue and 4% of the gross added value.

Guest Value
Are hotels aware of the value of their guests? I do not mean in euro revenue alone; I mean that every guest is an ambassador of the hospitality he / she is experiencing. Will he / she be a lobbyist for my hotel? Nowadays, guests have the power in their pockets. Much faster than you think, all good and bad experiences are shared by guests over smart

phones. It can be within seconds. So not only will the overall stay be reviewed, but everything that comes into the guest's minds will be posted right away. So do hotels know the main people whose opinions count, the influential people who stay in their hotels?

Family & Friends
Here some experiences that I have made by contacting hotel managers, sales & marketing managers, staff, etc. Mostly, when I book my room, I let the hotel know my profession and that I will write my personal view in my weekly blog. Some immediately "use" me and give me extra special treatment – not a massage or a bottle of champagne – no – the special treatment is that they want to be sure I get an authentic impression and all relevant information on the hotel; they are lobbying, and that is fine. In total, the most important experience I want to feel is, do I feel like I am at home? Do I feel welcome? Most hotels do lose many good contacts and partnerships to "opinion leaders" and to journalists, for example, by changing their management. It takes months and years to build up new partnerships. These do not cost a fortune but are so important to create a good atmosphere and to give the hotel an upfront bonus so bookings are more likely because these people will talk and write about you whether you like it or want it.

Destinations & European Union
It is the same with destinations. Do they know who is important? Do they know whom to talk to in their own country or even at the European Union? The car manufacturer industry or the pharmaceutical industry learned their lessons years ago and so laws and decisions have been made using their deep influence. It is not a question of morality it is a question of who will survive at the end.

Let's unite and be strong, let's spread our strength and make sure that we are heard.

Customer journey, use all touch points – Destinationcamp'12

© Martin Suiter

April 2012: In Hamburg, travel-, marketing-, sales-experts from all over Germany gathered at the 25hrs hotel conference room and listened to the keynote of Hasso von Düring (TUI board member) as opening speech of the 2012 Destinationcamp. Header: who has the power? Feeling powerless is just an excuse. Compared to corporate groups (top down) nowadays smaller and mid size companies can easily use the "wisdom" of the crowd. For large corporates the value added chain is breaking down and classic marketing strategies are dead. Social Sharing is the key to success. Use social media to access your client, to listen to him and communicate with him. Without this tool you are lost!

Some Stats from the latest Google survey for 2014:
72% will search and book through the Internet. Only 28% will be left for the travel agencies. 69.5% are not organised travellers. Important: 35% book for more than € 1.000,00 per trip. This is the fastest growing booking group with

+45%. To share the market you need to be absolutely customer oriented. 1-2 topics, clear positioning, information and booking technique is marketing.

More results from the Destinationcamp'12
Session days: In an intelligent manner, six sessions with different topics, each with a host and a mind mapper, were staged in the building of the ISM (International School of Management). An average of 20 people (80% always changed after each session) worked out thesis for the future strategies of tourism. Here are the results:

First of all: Tourism in Germany is more important to the economy than the car, machine building, and building industries. € 280 billion turnover, 2.9 million employees, 4.4% direct gross value equate to; let's be more self-conscious.

Key phrases are: follow the customer journey, use every possible touch point to "hook" your client. Be aware of where you come from, what your clichés are to build up your brand and be sexy when you are selling your capabilities. Last but not least, use your brain and your heart for innovation. Go from USP to ESP (Emotional Selling Proposition). But do not forget that you are doing business in an economic environment, so engage the local economy for your goals and integrate this in your strategies to promote your destination as a whole.

A concept, passion and self-confidence (be a rock star) is key to success.

Personal conclusion: it was a great experience once again, to feel the team spirit, to discuss with an open mind, sharing knowledge and experiences and generally having fun working together!

Food for Tourists – sensualize your destination

© Daniela Leonhard

If God would have wanted me to cook, why would he have built so many restaurants? You have the choice, especially on holiday. Thoughts about how food can sensualize a destination:

Not many places are trying to attract guests with their local food, as yet. But South Tyrol is the land of apples and wine as far as tourists are concerned. This worldwide fame has been fostered for more than 4 decades. We have all got those pictures in our head of farmers picking every one of their apples by hand and harvesting their wine with an inner passion, knowing that this product is native origin.

When you arrive in South Tyrol and see all the fruit fields and small villages, you feel comfortable being in a natural environment. Up to this point, nothing can destroy the inner warmth that you experience of being around "pure nature". In addition to this, because most tourists have been here several times, it feels like "coming home". Plus, most of you are travelling with friends and family. So South Tyrol covers the 3 most desired experiences that give each one of us joy and happiness: nature, home, family / friends.

How can people promote these influences?
Redrooster.it is a chain of producers of homemade products. Strictly controlled by the board and even the guests. Only the best products are allowed to advertise using the logo of the red rooster. More than 500 products such as wine, bread, herbs, eggs, cheese, apples, etc. are merchandised. Not every product is "bio", but is from an integrated

and controlled cultivation. Above all, you find agro-tourisms under that brand where you as a guest become a part of the family. Farmers have strong roots and are manufacturers in the truest sense of the word.

pursuedtirol.com is another market of "delights" and a creative way to bring local products to tourists and make them aware of the environment they are staying in. But this is not only for tourists, Pur Südtirol is nothing more than a neighbourhood store used also by the locals. Consumption of local food does not necessarily have to be expensive. With the philosophy of short distance delivery, synergies, innovations, complex developments and communication Pur Südtirol is able to keep prices lower and affordable. Nevertheless it is absolutely clear that this quality food cannot be offered at supermarket price levels.

These examples show that it can be valuable in many ways to sensualize your destination. To give it a desirable and passionate environment which is appreciable.

Is it all paradise, all harmony, all perfect? – No. With this extreme acreage, where most farmers have very few fields and are dependent on a good harvest, there is a strong necessity to protect the apples and grapes with hail nets and, of course, with chemical support. But there is no need to be afraid. The farmers are aware that customers, clients and tourists are very sensitive when it comes to this problem, so South Tyrol has its own laboratory that invents chemicals that do not harm the product and also take into account the health of the consumer. If you have any questions on this, call www.meranerland.com and ask for information and you will see how openly and honestly they deal with these serious / important questions.

What is the summary of all this? Yes – there is a big chance to promote your destination with local products, goods and services. But be aware that our social, openly "cross-linked" world is very sensitive to promises and marketing "tricks". Sooner or later cheating and lying will be unveiled and unmasked and there will be hardly any chance to recover.

KPMG or feel like home

Torrance Course, St. Andrews © Martin Suiter

In April 2012, KPMG unveiled their latest Golf Travel Insights 2012. There were a lot of interesting numbers and statistics that can help us understand the business of golf travellers. But what the numbers do not show is the warmth and the hospitality that golfers on the road (or even at home) expect. If you are on a journey, you evaluate the "quality" rating mostly on how much attention you received and how honest you felt that was. Personally, I hate that American-Collegiate-Supersmile that has no real meaning. But it is not the failure of the employees but rather the fact that the employer does not appear to care about their guests and therefore hire the wrong, insincere people.

The most important feeling of the people who deal with your guests should be: "I am a salaried employee and therefore it should be my personal business to see that our guests feel at home". The reason why I use "salaried" and "business" in that context is that employees must be aware that if they do not understand guest-hospitality as an integral part of their business, then they do not get any salary.

But can you teach hospitality? – No! If someone is not born with that instinctive feeling, then he or she should be working with machinery, for example, but not with people. But yes, you can sensitize for being open to guest demands. I strongly believe that you do not have to have the best, the most perfect, the nicest hotel, golf course, or similar. People will forget the little imperfections as long as they feel that their requirements or even their smallest complaints are taken seriously.

While you read this you might think "I know all that" – but does your behaviour reflect these demands? I mean, can you really say that is true, 24/7? Do all of your workers, employees and even partners who are in contact with your clients, understand and are clear on that point? If not, there are two ways of solving that spread. First, be prepared to fire the ones who are not willing to put your business first. Second, give the ones who are willing the support they need. This means, give them the understanding that you expect they should have for your guests.

Above all, travellers are your source of information. They have been to many other places and do not get tired of telling you about their experiences, whether they were good or bad. Listen to what they have to say and learn.

Use every statistic you learn about the "hard facts", and then be ready and well informed in order to take care of the wishes, requirements and demands of your guests. Be even more ready if you have failed for any reason in the past and let your guests feel that you are personally honoured that they are there. If you respect this, then you will change the statistics for the better yourself because then guests will come back more often to your place because they have felt understood – they have felt like they were "at home".

Tourism marketing needs strategies and working together

Netherlands © Martin Suiter

As a consultant for more than 20 years I meet clients again and again, who do want to invest in a new campaign, a new website or a new brochure but who do not have the courage to set up / start an outstanding project. I do not mean spend thousands of Euros. I mean to think about and brainstorm wide open and evolve a strategy that has a five-year perspective. To start such a development plan you have to know who you are, who your clients are, who your competitors are and last but not least who your partners could be. This is because we strongly believe that in a global world you cannot survive without the support of others. So even competitors can be your partners to start an outstanding campaign like www.the-alps.eu.

But even a small health village like Oberstaufen did two outstanding projects. One was "Oberstaufen+" where the price of one night in a hotel includes all activities like golf, mountain railway, swimming in the public pool, etc. The other idea was to become the first Google street view town in Germany. At a time when everybody complained about losing privacy with Google's street view project, the Oberstaufen marketing started thinking diversely and invited Google to launch their street view project in Oberstaufen. Google was so surprised that they did indeed start their project in Oberstaufen and that meant that Oberstaufen got a "free" marketing campaign worth millions of Euros.

Tourism & Solheim Cup

BMW PGA Championship 2010 © Martin Suiter

In the following I will give you my valuation (MPV – my personal view) about the staging of the Solheim Cup in Germany 2015. Yes, it is great to have a tournament of this dimension on German soil. Yes, there will be a lot of coverage all over the world. Yes, there will be about 100.000 spectators on that weekend in St. Leon-Rot. Yes, it will be typically German, absolutely 100% organised and a great show and atmosphere.

No, Germany is not yet prepared to make it a great business. Do not have the wool pulled over your eyes. Whether the Golf Club St. Leon-Rot (despite the fact that they had a European Tour Event years ago), nor the sponsors SAP / Allianz (it's not their business), nor the German Golf Federation nor its commercial company the DGS have ever experienced what it means to entertain a world audience for an event like that. Here, a holistic preparation is needed to involve all that will gain business out of an event like the Solheim Cup. You do not believe me? Let me prove myself right and ask anybody in the German tourism business, if they have ever heard about the Solheim Cup, the Ryder Cup, the Open, the Masters – the answer will be "No". Golf is not part of their incoming tourism business.

Well – there is a lot of educational work to be done to open the eyes of these people and gather facts to explain the value of so many corporates, hotels, guesthouses, fuel stations, restaurants, cultural locations / centers, etc. and last but not least get the people who live nearby motivated and to share the spirit of such a wonderful opportunity to advertise Germany. Get me right - we have the potential to be a golfing nation, but we need to wake people up and get them inspired. How can that be done? Involve companies who have worked for years in the tourism business and travel the world to invite everyone to come to Germany before 2015, in 2015 and after 2015. Every golfer who travels could be a potential ambassador. It is a fantastic chance to set new standards. Let's start now!

Golf

There is a lot of money in the golf market and it is very easy to exist there - is a wide spread opinion. But why is that market successful? Because most of the work that has been done was very well deliberated.

In golf, additional things that we all love, come together: a good story and many, many personal experiences. The English, the American and the Asian world dominate the sport of golf. In these markets there is the media interest. Most of the funds flow there; and only through these mass markets the rest can get a few crumbs from the "golf cake".

What I always criticize is that the market (especially in Germany) is greatly overestimated by the participants. Through this self-satisfied "we-are-good" mentality, there is a lack of the necessary pressure to develop the market for its own purposes. For a much better success there is no need in new players or more spectators. It needs less regulation, more openness to "foreign" interested persons and above all more unity.

PGAs of Europe, establishing the game of golf

The PGAs of Europe (PGAsE) is an association of national professional golfers associations. It represents, promotes and advises 32 European and 7 International PGAs on a business-to-business level. Its main focus is to improve the standards and opportunities in education and employment of golf professionals and based on this, ensure the excellence in the services provided by the PGA professionals.

The PGAsE has direct access to approximately 21.000 PGA professionals as well as indirect access to an audience of approximately 6.5 million amateur golfers.

PGA Professionals: Education & Employment
One of the main tasks is to monitor and evaluate educational programs of its member countries to oversee and set the standards. Different programmes for improving skills for PGA Professionals are another focus in the work of the PGAsE. In this context, the IPE programme (Initial Professional Education, a structured career path towards full PGA qualification) and the Coaches Circle (network between coaches of elite players and national coaches) should be mentioned.

Future plans of PGAsE
Preaching the attitudes and standards to the members is one thing, but setting these standards for their own work is another. This implementation is a top priority today as well

as in the future. For this reason, the PGAsE is currently running a strategic and brand-related restructuring in order to meet future challenges with optimal conditions.

Another process that is being implemented at the moment is the European Education Level System (EELS), a method of setting educational standards throughout the continent, taking into account the resources that the different national PGAs can deliver.

Conclusion
Communication and Networking is the key to success. Good to see that the PGAsE is working hard on this issue to improve and develop the game of golf!

MPV (my personal view)
When I was sitting as a Marketing Consultant at the PGAsE board table in the years 2004/2005 and we needed to discuss the use of the letters PGA, I learned a lot about the strength of this brand. In the end, we found the small "s" solution to be clearly identified as the umbrella organisation of the associated country PGAs. Also, I got to understand how the "political system" within a federation/ association works. Of course, as a fully capitalism oriented person, I needed to control my impatience. From today's perspective, I am still not a fan neither of these system nor organisations, but I understand the necessity of such systems. People like us, especially from the marketing and communication side want changes to be developed fast, but with these institutions and its braking effects some ideas are over thought, and most of the time that was good for the spirit of the game. Nevertheless, I plead for an involvement of opinion leaders and decision makers who are ahead of their time and have critical voices to keep ideas and innovation alive.

Solheim Cup – major chance?

Wentworth © Martin Suiter

GC St. Leon-Rot in Germany will be the host golf course for the 2015 Solheim Cup. Why? Did anybody else want it? Well, the Ladies European Tour struggles with their attractiveness. Plus, the European economy has put pressure on former hosts of LET events in general. Portugal, Spain and Italy are "dead", but also for the European Tour it is a huge challenge to be a "European" European Tour. Therefore it was relatively easy to bring the Solheim Cup to Germany, especially when the organisers are well experienced and with the backing of such strong main sponsors like SAP and Allianz. In addition, it is a lack of finance (LET gets the money) and organisation (Germans are world champions in that field) question in Germany.

It was still hard work, however, for Eicko Schulz-Hanßen, GM of St. Leon-Rot to get the backing for that event. "Ladies European Tour" does not have TV super star status and the efforts of the players are still not respected well enough in the world of sport. So why? I think they took it on as a challenge and they are aware that this jubilee Solheim Cup could be bigger than every cup before it. This goes together with the strong belief that they can achieve something big and the belief in the organisers own power. St. Leon-Rot, specifically, was always a pioneer in bringing golf closer to the people, to support young players (even with a major indoor facility), not only till they were on the Tour, but since this year far beyond with their own management strategies for Rookies. Later I am sure even Rory McIlroy could become a client.

This is proof that you do not cry for help and criticise your customers for not succeeding enough (like Günter O. Reiter, chief editor of GOLF Inside), did in February 2013 in his newsletter, and the announcement that the German GOLF Inside magazine will only be issued every two month from now on. In my opinion, the only person (except when natural disasters happen) to blame for not being able to keep yourself on any market is you! Especially in the print business, where alarms have been ringing for 2-3 years, and I bet (symbolic) that within the next two years, 50% of daily newspapers will not exist anymore in a printed version. And another bet is that 30% of all monthly magazines will disappear - either not exist or be transferred to a digital version.

Conclusion: Think of your own strengths, capabilities and ambitions and no one will be able to stop you! To me there is no question, that a host like St. Leon-Rot needs every support to be successful in staging this major event. Consequently, so many people will be winners if they succeed.

Golf and Image

BMW PGA Championship 2010 © Martin Suiter

It is time to send my MPV (my personal view) to comment on the incidents of November 2012. Yes, Germany can be very proud that Moritz Lampert made the QS to become a member of the European Tour. Yes, Germany can be very proud to have Caroline Masson, another player on the LPGA Tour. But is it due to the success of the German golf support system that these players have become successful? Well, again the answer must be yes, because both started their careers in the junior teams of the German Golf Federation. BUT why is it only one male player and one female player?

Well to give a correct answer, I think I must widen the perspective to look at this topic. Golf is still not the most popular sport in Germany. That does not help to recruit or interest new players to practise hard to become new stars. Golf has no role models for kids to say to themselves: "I can gain respect when I play golf". Golf is simply not cool enough. Plus with the thousands of options that kids have, it is hard to stick to such an intense sport. Plus, it is even harder to inspire and enthuse kids towards golf when the practise ground has no easy "bike-access". Last but not least, Germany must rethink the structure to support these kids who want to play golf. St. Leon-Rot is an excellent example of how this could work, plus, staging the Solheim Cup will have an impact. But golf would still need more money, more public funding to make it more attractive. Being an Olympic sport might help.

Golf still has no lobby. An extreme example is the disinvitation of Martin Kaymer on Europe's largest Saturday TV night show "Wetten, dass ...?". He was not the first choice. A man who was the world # 1, a man who has millions of fans worldwide; a man who is ambassador for Germany; a man who gained millions of Euros for the German economy. This is a clear indication that though golf is not considered "sexy" enough, he certainly is. A German newspaper mixed up his photos with a photo of Luke Donald, another top golfer. Are we aware that the image of golf is subterranean? But why? I think there are still too many SUVs on the parking lots at golf courses. This means golf has, for various reasons, not managed to be popular. It is not the number of players we must increase (but we should); the examples Biathlon and Ski jumping, just to name two, show that nobody needs to play a sport to find it attractive – for there are thousands at these events and millions on the couch in front of their TV.

One brick in the wall could be that golf becomes relevant to the German economy. At the moment, golf makes its revenues without public money. Golf has a great impact on the local economy. E.g. Golf brings thousands of tourists to Germany. So let's make a round table with all players in the market, plus decision makers from other countries and other branches so they can learn from each other and bring golf to a more acceptable level. Then I am sure we will see more players on either tour, who will be proud to be German golfers. And you never know, maybe one day the Olympic gold medallist will be a German. That would not be necessary for the pride of the Germans – that would be necessary to keep golf in Europe alive for all who are part of the game.

Ryder Cup and Journalism

© Martin Suiter

Europe won! Nobody would ever have expected that the Miracle of Medinah could possibly happen. But those journalists all wrote negative comments about the situation and especially about Martin Kaymer. It was typical journalism of our time. Again and again journalists, particularly those who have never played a competitive sport themselves, arrogate themselves to write their stories based on knowledge. We saw on Sunday how dramatically wrong these predictions and prejudgments can be. Just to state very clearly, I am talking about the small minority of journalists, not about the 15% true professionals and not about the 15% unenlightened who will fail forever.

My hope is that we all are aware of the strength of the written and spoken word. Nobody can assume how an outcome of a sporting event will be before the last putt is struck or until the game is over. We are not gods. We are obliged to report about what we see, hear and feel and we need to say that all assumptions are just our personal opinion about what might happen. Also personal attacks on coaches, players, board members, people in charge need to be made with respect, not "below the belt" and on the understanding that nobody can empathize from outside. The decision makers are influenced by so many factors and have such individual manners and behavior that it is simply impossible to judge the determination of that player, coach, ...

And finally – we as Europeans have the liability to protect our business and to be ambassadors. These athletes did not only win for themselves they won for "Golf in Europe", for all of us working in this industry – so please – more enthusiasm, more anticipation, more optimism for the sake of the game and for the sake of all of us.

Wi-Fi and Thunder – devastating the game of golf

Merano, Suedtirol © Martin Suiter

In June 2012, we started asking two questions to the online community. The following will give you the results and the outcome and leave you with some good advice regarding Wi-Fi on the course and the weather.

Is it reasonable to offer Wi-Fi on the golf course? A very controversial discussion. Many people responded and were divided on this subject. Here are some extracts of their comments: It is a must in order to attract more younger players to the game. Kids want to share their experiences right away and post pictures to their friends. Plus they do not want to be distracted from their "society". Others say that phone access should be unavailable and phones turned off, because it is too annoying for the other flight partners receive calls. Players should enjoy the company of their flight partners more. If you need to use Wi-Fi, stay in the clubhouse! On the other hand, carts with Wi-Fi could receive messages from the clubhouse and Pro Shop. Examples; how is the cart traffic? (speed up your game) or to order your 9 hole lunch or more importantly, the weather warning (see below). At the end you could send your score directly to your social media accounts.

The tragic lightning incident in Germany was followed by many comments on the issue: The most asked questions were – does the owner, the management or the tenant have responsibility for the shelters, facility constructions or is the shelter owned by the golf course? Many said that they have big signs in the clubhouse that make it clear how to behave "in case of lightning …". Some have early weather warnings with sirens to get people off the course. Some even send out staff to pick up everybody who is still out there. The most common advice was that there should be an additional sign in the shelter that says if (or if not) the shelter is built to be safe in case of heavy weather conditions. But one thing is clear; the management has to contact the weather stations well in advance to see if there is some bad weather coming up in order to protect their guests and members.

My Personal View (MPV) in the question of Wi-Fi is that I like to play without my smart phone switched on, and not to distract people who are playing the game. However, we need to be open minded to everybody who does keep their mobiles on. But there should still be a sign on the first tee that asks you to turn mobiles off and so you can enjoy the game more with your flight partners in this quieter environment. The lightning issue made it clear that every club has to take heed of their own duties and responsibilities to provide the highest possible safety for the players. Do not be too easy-going with issues that could have serious impact on the health of people who are out there on the course. In addition, get legal advice who is ultimately responsible for any damage compensation.

Wi-Fi on course – stay connected

BMW PGA Championship 2010 © Martin Suiter

In June 2012, we ran a poll about Wi-Fi on the golf course. It was amazing how many people from the golfing industry replied, and it was interesting to read their controversial discussions. A summary could be that most of them accept Wi-Fi as a "must- have" to attract more players, especially younger ones, but many would personally prefer to stay disconnected during their game. That affirms the organisers of The Open. Where phones and smart phones were strictly banned last year, and this year they were allowed. I think it will have a very negative effect. Spectators will not watch the game with their own eyes and most of them will see it through their smart phones – what for?

However, "the Open" will be flooded with spectators, in contrast with to the BMW Intl. Open in Cologne 2012. Despite the strong players on the field, despite the BMW advertising; despite the fact that there are thousands of golfers around

Cologne; despite the good results and Marcel Siem fighting for the lead; despite the changing leaders; there were only a few golfers who wanted to see the efforts of the players live on site on Sunday. Why is that? OK, one point could be due to the bad weather, but can you imagine only a few people sitting in the Grand Stand on an Open Sunday? Could it be that the online coverage – (I keep myself informed wherever I am and whatever I am doing) is having a negative effect? Especially in countries that are not addicted to golf?

Nevertheless we cannot stop online "life". So we should deal with it.

Golf & Emotions survey results or: What characterizes a golfer?

The target group of golfers is very special and complex: people between 18 and 80, men and women, all with different education levels and incomes. But one thing unites them: the fascination of golf!

The question is: who is he / she - the golfer? What characterizes and touches her / him?

Our golf survey, with 1079 participants, is showing what golfers really feel and expect on and off the golf course. The most interesting findings were that golfers do expect little things that do not cost a fortune to satisfy their needs as customer. Example, 43% said that they would like to compete in a tournament at a time that is convenient for them. 42% said that slow play is a nightmare. The most accepted and used reduction of green fee promotions is 2for1.

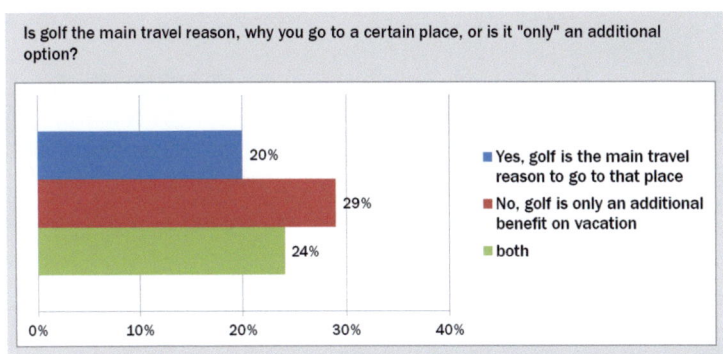

Is golf the main travel reason, why you go to a certain place, or is it "only" an additional option?

- Yes, golf is the main travel reason to go to that place: 20%
- No, golf is only an additional benefit on vacation: 29%
- both: 24%

MS-Co Survey "The Golfers Heart" 2009

So what do we need to learn from that survey?

First: keep it simple = reduce friction. Give your clients sufficient access to your course, hotel, company, etc. Be open and authentic!

Second: Golf is not everything in life. Take that as an opportunity to gain partners. Golfers do use the whole environment. They go to restaurants; they are interested in culture and local habitats, classic and modern concerts and events. So if golfers come to your establishment there is a big share of this consumer for all kinds of business. Let's connect!

Third: Talk and listen to your customers. Golfers tell you everything you want to know and more. You can learn from their experiences at other hotels, destinations and courses, what they have experienced at corporate events, etc. and what they like or what they would improve. Listen and learn!

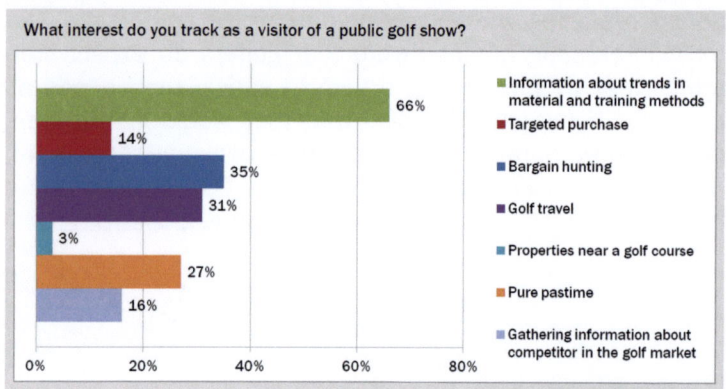

MS-Co Survey "The Golfers Heart" 2009

BMW Int. Open – time for change

BMW PGA Championship 2010 © Martin Suiter

The BMW International Open (BIO) staged from 21st to the 24th of June 2012 for the first time in history of this tournament in Cologne. Why was that? Well, it was time for a change. After 22 years of consecutive upswing success in Munich Eichenried, the BIO needed some refreshment. But as the only European Tour Event in Germany it was clear that we shouldn't leave the country just the location and so Gut Lärchenhof near Cologne was found as an alternating host course, before the BIO returns to Munich for one year and then goes back to Cologne again in 2014. BMW is an international car manufacturer that gains a part of its marketing recognition through the sport of golf. Martin Kaymer the former #1 player was the brand ambassador (till 2013) and BMW has put him into the right spot to be ever present.

Visitors and sponsors

Cologne will give BMW clients the chance to see BMW golf sport nearby, this time in the North. Thus, BMW becomes closer to their customers and golf fans. Plus BMW gets new sponsors out of that "new" region. This means new business partners, new challenges, new ideas. Also the sponsors will have the chance to use the BMW brand to gain new prospective customers and invite their clients to one of the top sporting events in Germany. Furthermore, there were new pictures sent out around the world. Everybody wants to see the players facing new competitions with the new course they now have to deal with. And to be honest, the Eichenried golf course was never a really challenging course which to my mind should it be to the players. There is nothing more boring than a winner with double figures under par.

BMW / YOU

What can we learn from this strategy? Be refreshing. Stay interesting. Give all integrated partners new ideas to think about. And if this is done in a calm way and with a "working together" atmosphere you will see how many will jump on the "car" to drive towards a new era. From my point of view I hope it will be a success, because all the people in this business need companies like BMW who feel encouraged enough to put a lot of money into the pot and have the guts to try something different.

Is Golf in Europe united?

Wentworth © Martin Suiter

I read an online article by Michael Lenihan published in Golf Management Europe – April 2012, which really attracted my attention. It draws a very critical view on the 2012 European Golf Business Conference, hosted by the EGOCOA (European Golf Course Owners Association).

Lenihan criticizes the choice of the location, which is the seventh conference not taking place at a golf venue with the following words "the EGCOA is doing the industry a great disservice" and "the EGCOA and its conference are in serious danger of losing all credibility".

2013 the conference is taking place at the Hotel Majestic Barriere in Cannes, which, again, is no golf resort or has anything to do with golf at all. I can totally share Lenihan's opinion on that. How can such an important golf association make such crucial mistakes – not for the first time but for the seventh?

Lenihan ends his article with the following questions:
"Why is a conference designed to help put money in the coffers of golf clubs not helping to put money in the coffers of golf clubs? Isn't it about time that an event that "seeks to address issues of common interest to all levels of the golf industry" started leading by example?"

My MPV (My Personal View) is that as long as not every European Body accepts that we need to unite all the power that we have in Europe we will be not as strong as we deserve to be. It is not only the EGCOA it is also the German Golf-Congress in Nuremberg for example, that should be part of Golf Europe and maybe even extended as a European Golf-Conference; the PGAsE AGM should be staged at alternate venues in one of its member countries; etc.

The European borders are open but minds are still closed – let's take the next step and cope with the extraordinary achievements of the European Tour Players.

Develop new golf course marketing ideas

Achensee © Martin Suiter

Every Course Manager promotes his course with stunning views, perfect greens and a good restaurant no matter if it is true or not. Is this enough to persuade us to come and play on that course? What is the difference to other courses?

I think you need a direct approach to the green-fee players you want to see on your course. You want these players not only wanting to play your course but they should also understand how to play that course. When I play a course for the first time I pay too much attention to where to play and to orientate myself. After the 18th I think often to myself that I would play this course totally differently the second time.

This is the reason why you should offer to buy, with the green-fee, a second green-fee (2 for 1). Tell the players: "our course has some tricky holes, but you will experience it in a really different way. Because we know that we offer you that 2 for 1 green fee, if you can be here again within the next 10 days." What is the effect of that? The guests receive valuable information from you. He will take more care, buy some more balls in the Pro-Shop and, to show you are concerned about him / her, you make a fair offer and the guests will feel already welcome to come back the second time.
But even you will gain benefits from that offer. Instead of the players going to play somewhere else, they come back to

your course. If you're lucky, even better if with a friend. He feels flattered and drinks another beer, filled with excitement. He opens up and tells you about his requirements and experiences elsewhere. The short time range of 10 days enables you to remember this guest and you can then target him specifically.

How to legally help golfers to improve:
I think you should give your members and guests (once a month or year), the super-chance of improving their handicap. Why not consciously and by announcing it, make the course easier? The tees on the tee boxes at the very front, the flags in the middle of the green, marked clearly GUR, cut widely critical fairway bottlenecks etc. But also involve your Pro, who can exclusively explain how to best play the course before teeing off.

As well as this, you can "rock the boat" with a Super-Challenge-Day where you prepare the course to be as difficult as possible once a year. But also on this more difficult course, the Pro should give help to enable players to cope. Men will be excited because they love to be challenged, but even ladies will come and try to face up to the challenge which will naturally stir up the men even more. In the evening you will need to "loosen up" the situation, because most of the players won't have played their handicap and will complain, frustrated about what went wrong that day. You will hear them say: "Next time I will play that course differently." Announce that you are so excited about the players who have faced the challenge that you will invite them all for dinner and drinks (or at least, drinks). What effect do you think will that have?

Summarized – what will be the effect of both ideas? Only if you are able to attract interest your course will be talked about. Only when you manage to engage people you are able to create emotions. Golfers will talk about your course, about the experiences they had, about the hospitality. And you are perfect when you have gathered all these emotions before and after such an event on various social media platforms.

The struggle of the Ladies European Tour

Connemara, Ireland © Martin Suiter

The Ladies European Tour is struggling. There are no investors in sight who want to invest in a highly attractive environment. Why attractive? Sex sells and what could be more attractive than well-dressed girls with sporty elegance. Another plus is that an engagement for investors would be affordable. But what has to be changed, in my opinion, it is the fact that relying on nice looking girls is not nearly enough.

The tour needs media presence and there is a comparable situation for all golf "institutions" on the continent. A four-day tournament is too long, the quality of the players is too low and there is a personality like Nadal, Vettel, etc. missing. How can we change that? A new strategy for the next five years is needed and the sport needs support from the very successful European Tour.

Why not mix certain tournaments with the top five ladies and the top five amateurs? Why not have a 1 Mio. Euro shoot out?

The Golf Live event is an excellent example of bringing golf to the people. However, every single federation has to do its homework. The sponsor has to commit more than by just bringing the money to the table. Plus, they should support junior golf, but not pamper the youngsters and demand full engagement. The absolute focus for these kids must be "I want to become a top five Tour Player".

A great example for the right approach to drawing the right attention and to get something started is the Million Dollar Invitational, took place in 2012 in Carrick on Loch Lomond.

The article "An LPGA Tour player finds out how golf really treats women" by Peter Finch in the March issue of the "Golf Digest" magazine also started a heated discussion on the topic "golf and women". The online editorial department even reacted with its own blog post on the numerous comments and a lively discussion also started on their Facebook page. The article can be found via golfdigest.com

Golftimer vs. mobile App

© Martin Suiter

During the last years, all print-media circulations have been constantly decreasing. Why is that? We're not only moving inside the virtual world by using our computer or laptop. On the one hand, the new smart phones and tablets enable us to be online wherever and whenever we want. On the other hand, we are forced to carry all our knowledge with us.

The difference between the past and the present is that we are now able to do this. The massive growth of information – what we know, what we should know and what we should be able to answer – we need access to supply that information immediately when somebody (client, boss, family) is asking for it.

Can you imagine keeping somebody waiting with the words: "Hold on, I need to go to my office, where I can find the magazine, encyclopaedia, catalogue, and federation data base or similar on the bookshelf?" No, those times are definitely over. Your questioner (or "demander") needs and wants the answer right now, this second. So what are you going to do? You are prepared, you are online and with the right App or search engine you can cope with the requirements of your opponent right away.

Hence, this trend will not stop in the future business world. Pupils will not have to carry a heavy school bag any more. They will have their iPad or, even better, they will have one at school and one at home, where all the information will be saved in the Cloud. Anytime, anywhere. All they (pupils) have learned and what they have to learn will be available, including current news around the world. The best – no more back pain from their school bag. You think that this the future scenario? Did you know that some schools are already testing it? One excellent example for the usage of iPads in schools is the Kaiserin Augusta School in Cologne.

I am absolutely convinced that there is no going back to the illusion of a sheltered and convenient publishing sector. Even the orthography will be of minor importance because the only thing that will matter is the message itself. Going into exact detail will only be important for specialists, scientists, researchers etc. We, as the usual consumers, will be inundated with information from all our gadgets, apps, newsrooms, social media platforms, etc. and we will only be able to capture the headlines but not the content. If we search for something in particular we need fast – super fast – personalised filters. This means the search engine knows my personal habits, needs and behaviour patterns to give me the exact search results for what I am looking for at that moment, or even better, knows what I will be looking for.

According to a recent study of G.K.M.B. smart phone and tablet users who access golf club websites via their mobile devices are increasing to above-average numbers. The MARTIN SUITER – Consultancy also started a survey on its social media platforms. The results are clearly showing the movement from print to mobile; approximately 23% would still prefer to buy a printed version whereas 77% would clearly prefer the mobile application.

I personally think that the time for a database like the Golftimer is definitely over. Why is the German Golf Federation not investing in an up to date App, which consists of all the actual data, contact details, links, etc. In my opinion this would make it much more efficient when it comes to golf data sharing within Germany. Mobile applications are the way forward and not even the Golftimer can deny that.

George O´Grady about the Ryder Cup bid 2018

Portmarnock, Ireland © Martin Suiter

At the event "The Open" in 2011, I had the chance to talk to George O'Grady, Chief Executive of The European Tour, and asked him for an explanation why Germany did not got the Ryder Cup 2018.

Here is what he said, written from memory:

Germany always wants to deliver an outstanding performance and deliver a Masterpiece. But we just asked for security, which means:

1.) We wanted to be sure about the course we would be playing on. The danger with a "to-be-built" course is, if any Roman reliquaries were found, that could have delayed the construction, we might have been in trouble. In France the infrastructure is already there and the course has been proven by tournaments being played.

2.) We wanted to be very close to a major city. Berlin or Munich would have been perfect.

3.) The governmental support and the support of all golfing fans is another issue that we had to consider.

4.) Support for the "not-yet-golfers" and the kids was crucial. For example Gleneagles, Scotland made sure that every kid in the age group of 5 to 8 had a golf club in his hands at least once.

He ended with some hope for Germany: Germany will get the Ryder Cup some day. Not necessarily in 2022, but 2026 could be an option.

Franciacorta – playing golf in Italy

© Franciacorta

I had the pleasure of playing at Franciacorta. The course is located near Brescia and just 30 minutes from the south end of Lake Garda. As you see in the picture, it has magnificent colours of autumn at this time of the year.

Who needs an Indian Summer, when you can play at a place like this?

My recommendation is to play 9 holes at the "Brut" and 9 at the "Saten" course. The 9 at "Rosé" are fairly new and might need one more season to "grow".
But not only is the Rosé new, the whole Range has been refurbished and is now ready and in optimal condition for improving your game.

Two more suggestions: when playing for the first time, take advantage of a "yardage book" or one of those new gadgets to show you around + be aware that they have 160 tournaments a year so book in advance. In Italy, however, you can play on a tournament day without participating. It is just a matter of space. After the game you can get revitalized by all what they have to offer in the Clubhouse or you can hop on the car and drive a few minutes further to enjoy the stunning surroundings of Lago d'Iseo.

Contact details:
Franciacorta Golf Club, Via Provinciale 34/b, 25040 Nigo-line di Corte Franca (BS)
+39-030-984167, segreteria@franciacortagolf.it

Communication & Social Media

Talk, talk, talk – this was present even before the development of the speech centre. Since its origin, communication is socially predisposed. Even the hermit communicates at least with himself.

Today, we could come into contact with the whole world in the much-cited sense. Meaningful communication differs from background noise, which already makes us sick sometimes. To prevent this filtered listening from the outset is important. If I know what it is and the issue is defined, the experience to deal with it is needed. Finally, a creative spirit that guides everything into targeted tracks with minimal wastage.

I am convinced that we are at the very beginning of the development of the virtual and viral world. If you consider that the knowledge of the NSA is not yet incorporated in the markets, you cannot imagine or even know what companies will develop with these mass profiles or of individuals, in order to benefit from the consumer-economy-growth-cycle. This is probably the reason why everything just rushes past us so that we could counter neither the current possibilities nor the future questioning. In order to deal with this, stay cool and try to surprise your customers and partners with innovations.

© Daniela Leonhard

In September 2011, we entered the world of Social Media. One goal of the Social Media strategy is to deliver free and fast access to sport & tourism information via different social media channels. As a fan and follower of our channels, you will be part of an exclusive group that receives information about the latest developments in the realm of the sport of golf and premium tourism. Furthermore, we are running a corporate blog, which contains MPVs (my personal views) of Martin Suiter on topics such as travel patterns, golf business and leisure attitudes. The hard facts until now:

Facebook Friends & Fans: 763
Twitter Follower: 211
Blog Readers: average of 250 readers per month
LinkedIn contacts: 576
Xing contacts: 332
(Figures from February 2014)

We know that we do not do everything right in this field and we are learning day by day, but we are on the right track as our numbers show.
Why?

Content – is the simple answer! Instead of boring people with breakfast pictures or pictures of the construction process of a private home, we share our knowledge, we share our contacts and we send information of "good-to-know" facts that helps to improve and create more business. Plus, we do it in a personal way, means we send MPVs (My Personal Views) so we do not indoctrinate people, but we let them know what, in our opinion and our 20 years of experience, is interesting and state of the art in marketing, communication and networking in the field of sport and tourism.

We work very well with many agencies, hotel chains, federations, corporations and many more, and we often find a very cooperative way and understanding of give-and-take. However, some (example tourist organisations or hotels) do indeed send information, but do not want to know what we thought of it, how we used it or how we promoted their interests. Often they do not "like" us, they never ask what happened or what was the outcome – there seems to be no will to improve but merely to execute what she or he is told to.

Why?

To be honest, I think there are too many non-professionals out there. We strongly recommend that owners, CEOs, managers, dismiss these people or revise them more intently and inhale them the spirit of the corporation. But that is sometimes the key point; the management itself is not capable and has no personal stance.

So why are we successful? We love what we do and we fully engage with our duties and with our client's mission.

Review communication congress Berlin

Rüdiger Grube, CEO of Deutsche Bahn AG © Martin Suiter

The communicating family met at the communication congress in Berlin 2012. Here we summarised the highlights of the two days with 1.600 participants from PR to Marketing.

Opening Keynote by Rüdiger Grube, Deutsche Bahn AG: Part of the strategy is communication – listening and talking with each other, being as close as we can be to the customers of this corporate with 230.000 employees. Social Media is a big challenge, because people want to see a "big player" like this fail. The audience agreed that Mr. Grube was very authentic and a man who could be trusted.

Video as a promotion tool: Be aware that video is a great tool, but do not overestimate it. A live stream of a car presentation (Audi) e.g. was only of real interest for 3 minutes, then the number of online live viewers declined intensely. Also, the Click-Through-Rate (CTR) to the website is rather low. Use the cliff hanger effect to enhance this (e.g. "how does the story end? See our website!"). See Forrester Research for more studies and stats. In addition, you could get more stimulation on Daily Motion or even 56.com. Another idea would be if you put together a slideshow with information and add pictures and some music and published that as video. See more on: Animoto / Go 2 Web / Tech Smith. One last point: use videos inside communities of shared interest!

Brand communication by Dr. Oetker: 96% know this brand; 63% find it very satisfactory; 63% like the use of the products – all activities are done on the premises. No agencies, marketing or PR companies are involved. This gives total control and the success underlines that strategy: Their own "Back-Club" has 100.000 members.

Brand communication by Jacobs: The DNA of the brand is that Jacobs brings people together. "Let's have a coffee". Plus, their strategy is to cooperate with the Allensbach Institute, a research company that is backing the development of our ageing society. There are a lot of editorials about the studies Jacobs does with that institute so people see and read about the effort that is made to care about our society as a whole. Europe's largest women's magazine "Bild der Frau" is official media partner and underlines the social engagement of Jacobs. The keywords are: inspirational, involving, activating.

Last but not least: The controversial scientist Prof. Dr. Manfred Spitzer talked about creativity and luck. He said: You must have knowledge to be creative! We perceive things by 1/3rd using our eyes and 1/3rd using movement. In addition, (walking in nature) we hold information easier. If you have good, positive feelings you learn faster and you develop more creativity. But without surprises you do not learn, because you do not have any feelings of happiness. A permanent feeling of happiness is impossible. We need surprises to have these feelings again and again. One key factor he maintains is that only with knowledge are you able to "google", if you do not have any background knowledge, the results on Google will make no sense. What was interesting was that men under a MRT do reflect immediately when they see pictures of a Porsche. They don't, however, by seeing pictures of a Daihatsu.

Social Media – Best Case

Gombm Alm, Suedtirol © Martin Suiter

Careful – it sounds so easy to write for or to take over Social Media coverage from a client. And in the first place it is if your client is willing to go forward and not blocking you by every innovative way of writing. Because Social Media blogging is not editing an article for any magazine or paper. Social Media gives you the chance to be much, much closer to your clients and it is a mutual way of conversation / communication. That offers an intercommunication where both sides are learning, improving and experience listening. So your client's product or service can spontaneously be changed or adopted to those useful thoughts.

But you need to clarify and state very clear what your challenges / your duties are. We do not recommend mixing it with your existing networks to promote your clients social networks. At the end nobody can separate the different platforms and intentions. The pictures you will send should have an unprofessional touch to be more authentic. You are not producing usual "clean" PR stuff. People want to see how it is there (e.g. exhibition) right now to be able to get a real impression with these fleeting glimpses.

The most difficult part is during and after (e.g. exhibition). The impressions of the visitors differ sometimes dramatically from the impressions the exhibitors have, because there are different intentions on both sides. Plus the intention of the organizers must be respected, but as I said the personal perception inveigled readers, posters, ... to comment in a subjective manner. You need to constantly control what the community reports and you need to be able to interfere when the mood or the way of complaining is going an unacceptable way. Invite the protesters to get in touch with you directly and that you are willing to listen to arguments and that you want to improve and to learn from the complaints.

Bad critics are written in comments but good comments are only given in "likes". If you want to have these good and positive commentaries you need to "push" people to do so. They usually do not come automatically. Finally from client side it must be clear that your mission / contract end one day and the client has to take over.

Survey about social media and travel

Dubai © Martin Suiter

Survey social media/travel made by Faber Touristik Consulting and FH Worms with 4.000 employees from airlines, hotels, destinations, travel agencies:

Summarised it's remarkable that almost no one has a social media strategy. So it does not amaze me that many companies do moan about the view results they perform with social media. An outstanding number for example is that most travel agencies do not get access to the under 35s, but this group does own 30% of the whole travel market. They would be easy to catch because on a day by day basis these people contact 3-4 communities and 81% would book online immediately, but only 15% would in a travel office.

The results in detail: Touristic entrepreneurs are Internet affine, so use more than 50% smart phones. 73% do have the permission of their employer to be social media active at their desk. But for 69% it is a no-go receiving advertisement. 48% do have an own Facebook page, 33% do have a twitter account and 23% use Google places. But only a view use sustainable platforms like weblogs. 71% admit that they do not have a strategy and so it is clear that only 15% control what is written about them and only 30% spend more than 5 hrs per week to maintain their social media presence.

Airlines (77 worldwide): 91% of them do have an own Facebook website and 12% are even in German language. They do have an average of 42.679 fans, but 47% less than 1.000 fans. 65.2% do write on a regular basis. 87% do have a twitter account with an average of 18.158 followers. 50.7% do have on YouTube canal with an average of 38 videos and 427.793 uploads.

Hotel brands (94 worldwide): 74.5% of them do have an own Facebook website and have an average of 6.161 fans. 46% have posted 5 messages within the last 14 days. 24.3% use existing Apps and connect them with their page. 52% are on twitter with an average of 4.345 followers. 52.1% do use an own YouTube canal with an average of 21 videos and 127.759 uploads.

Travel organizers (252 in Germany): 56.3% do have a Facebook page as a sub page with an average of 2.162 fans. 36.1% have a twitter account with an average of 751 followers. 25% have their own YouTube channel with an average of 38.863 uploads.

Appendum from the 15th of November 2011:
- 70% of the U.K. golfers rely on their friend's recommendations where to take a golf break.
- 43% rely on their golf professional
- 35% on blogs and course reviews
- Research also revealed that 36% (more than a third) do research their last golfing holiday on social media websites. Almost half of the 30-year-olds did. A quarter of all did change the hotel were due to stay in based on social media reviews.

The message is – that everyone can be an ambassador or influencer for your business, so you must ensure that your product, service and customer experience is outstanding and memorable for all the right reasons.

- Golfers with handicap 5 and below travelled most likely to long haul destinations, especially the US & UAE
- Third of the golfers surveyed who have been on an international golf break stayed most recently in self-catered accommodation, making the number one accommodation type
- Over half of the golfers surveyed (52%) book their international golf breaks between six and twelve months in advance of their departure dates

All numbers and stats with courtesy of www.touristikconsulting.de, Markus Faber, 2011.

Exhibition

If you have helped shape, create and have lived through many fairs and events, you always think you have seen everything. But on this subject, even I can still be mistaken and I am amazed time and time again. But extensive experiences protect us from unnecessary mistakes, or at least from expensive mistakes.

It is a field that depends immensely on human interaction from all who are involved. Again, the unifying objective is on focus. Enthusiasm will attract the audience, therefore everyone involved must also have enthusiasm, which lets us believe irrefutably in success, but at the same time, not be blind to one's own fallibility.

Overconfidence is in many areas of economic life the "nail that closes the coffin of dreams."

Exhibition season – Do's and Don'ts

IMEX 2012 © Martin Suiter

In autumn, the exhibition season and conference season is about to come. With more than 20 years of exhibition experience I want to make you aware of the do's and don'ts of exhibiting and visiting. Below you will find the links to a number of recommended exhibitions.

In general exhibitions and conferences are the melting pot of knowledge and the places for analogue networking. Touching people, looking in their eyes, gaining information first hand and feeling the mood of a whole industry or branch; that is what you can only get when you are there. No digital instrument or gadget will be able to replace that. Doesn't matter if you are an exhibitor or a visitor.

You as an exhibitor – there are a number of questions that you should look into. You want to exhibit? What do you have to exhibit? Are you prepared for all the questions that may come? Do you have a crew who is engaged in selling your product or service? Why did you choose this event?

You as a visitor – in times of strict reduction in expenses you should evaluate exactly why the exhibition or conference is of paramount importance for you to be there in person and how many hours / days you want to spend there. Not only the show hours are important, but also the social occasions and meetings are the key for collecting information and to get closer to your partners and even to your competitors. Sometimes, while having a beer at the bar opportunities arise that you might never have dreamed of. But you need to be prepared. Who will attend, what do I want to gain or achieve? You need to be present with 120% engagement to be able to see and take up any opportunities.

Tips and Tricks:

As an exhibitor – apply very early. This will enable you to get the best spot and use the earliest possible advertising. Talk to the exhibition project management about additional possibilities of advertising, marketing, positioning, comments in press releases or exhibition magazines. Do a speech, workshop, presentation, lecture, to get extra attention and to contact the visitors in more sophisticated surroundings. Buy the maximum of sponsor package to intimidate your competitor. Use professional PR and make yourself visible on all platforms.

As a visitor – be prepared. Get connected on all possible platforms to all possible conversational partners. Organise a social party in the evening at another venue in order to get the chance to speak privately with people who you are interested in.

As an exhibition organiser – listen to your clients. Use synergies with exhibitors and visitors. Deliver content. Be transparent with prices and your goals. Use Social Media to enable you to be present all year round. Use experts, opinion leaders, ambassadors to lobby for your event, congress, fair, …

One of a kind – the CBI 2012

Martin Suiter and Carsten Sühring © Remigius Heubuch

The largest golf consumer show "Golf & WellnessReisen" took place for the 18th time at the CMT trade fair in Stuttgart in 2012. The successful mix of travel, sales and events was once more a magnet for around 30.000 visitors and more than 270 exhibitors.

That year the MARTIN SUITER – Consultancy was the proud host of the Creating Business Invitational that took place for the first time. The goal was to create a one-of-a-kind B2B platform, where professionals get inspired, synergies will evolve and new co- operations can be developed. Last Friday, top communication, marketing and sales managers had the possibility to present their company and latest projects to an exclusive group of participants. The unique concept behind it was: 1 hour + 6 project presentations + 20 experts = CBI 2012

Hereinafter a short summary of the Creating Business Invitational 2012:

After the opening remarks by Martin Suiter, the chief editor of GOLF TIME Oskar Brunnthaler presented details of the development of his magazine over the last 15 years as well as the need of diversification strategies in the publishing industry. Followed by Marco Hauprich, the Mobile & New Media director of HRS, who informed the participants of the CBI 2012 about the most current development in the mobile market with a special focus on the success story of the HRS mobile application. Matthias Weidner, sales manager at DHL, introduced the market potential of innovative e-commerce services in his presentation. The tourism consultant Konstantin Andreas Feustel presented the ground-breaking marketing concept "Oberstaufen+" which created an incredible additional value for the guests and therefore rapidly increased the bookings. The next presentation of the CBI 2012 was held by the general manager of Stuttgart Marketing, Armin Dellnitz, about the creative new branding concept of the Region Stuttgart instead of only focusing on the city Stuttgart. Mr. Sühring, sales manager Hapag Lloyd Cruises challenged the participants with the question of how a new premium lifestyle product can be credibly combined with the long history and tradition of the company.

Review of the IGTM 2011

IGTM 2011 © Martin Suiter

The IGTM'11 (International Golf Travel Market) made a stop in Belek, Turkey. From 13th to 18th November 2011 this was the meeting point for all IAGTO (International Golf Tour Operators) members including the IGTWA (International Golf Travel Writers Association) members worldwide.

Belek is comprised of golf and hotels, nothing more, but also nothing less. Excellent courses and 5 star hotels edge the south coast of Turkey about 40 minutes drive east of Antalya airport. When you drive there, sitting in a bus or taxi, it is similar to a drive by train down the Nile. Where there is water, there is prosperity, wealth and cleanliness. However, on the other side of the bus, taxi or train there is the desert and poverty. We were there for work, however.

Sadly enough, on the tournament, it was pouring with rain and it was cold on Monday. So some of us played either no golf, 3 holes, 9 holes or very few of us al 18. Tuesday, the first of three exhibition days, we had to enter the buses that drove us 40 minutes back to Antalya exhibition centre which was mainly a huge hall not decorated in any particular style. The food corner was in the open-air and due to the low temperatures we felt never warm or welcome.

I do not know if it was Reed or the local provider, but nobody made much effort when serving the members, buyers, writers, exhibitors. Everything was done in a half-hearted way – carpets, lights, even the pre-booked Wi-Fi did not work as it should have done at an event like that. Nevertheless, we were there to do business and not to complain about the circumstances. It was productive, and for most of the participants, it was successful.

I would like to mention that the atmosphere between the suppliers, buyers, writers, competitors was remarkable and that is the way we should all work these days – hard working and competitive but at the end be cheerful and enjoy a beer. All the functions and receptions, official and not so official, were well organised, done with good sentiment and had good vibes. And of course, as it is the usual way – some deals were finalized at the bar. So on the flight home, reflecting on the week in Belek, it was almost essential to participate in IGTM, therefore, I will pack my suitcase again for IGTM'12 in the Algarve. Further information, comments and pictures can be found on Facebook and Twitter.

Appendix

After reading this book you shared some of my thoughts and views. But it was not only my phantasy, my concepts, my creativity, it is a compendium of my personal experience combined with lots of thoughts / ideas others developed and shared with me. Last but not least I point out the inspiration I got from many books and studies that I have read over the last 10 years to understand how we humans evolved and behave like we behave.

"First learn behaviour, than study."
sign on the entrance of the Literature Temple, Hanoi, Vietnam

Book Tip = must read

"Thinking, Fast and Slow" by Daniel Kahnemann

Useful Links from references in this book

Animoto: www.animoto.com
A-ROSA: www.a-rosa-golf.de
BIO: www.bmw-golfsport.com
Daily Motion: http://www.dailymotion.com
DestinationCamp: www.destinationcamp.com
D-Hotel Maris: www.dhotel.com.tr
EIBTM: www.eibtm.com
Franciacorta: www.franciacortagolf.it
Gasthof Hirschen: www.hotel-hirschen-bregenzerwald.at
Golf- & WellnessReisen: www.cmt-golf.de
Golf Business Forum: www.golfbusinessforum.com
Golf Digest: www.golfdigest.com
Golf Live: www.celtic-manor.com/the-celebrity-cup-2014
Guestmob: www.guestmob.com
Hotel München Palace: www.hotel-muenchen-palace.de
Hotel Post Bezau: www.hotelpostbezau.com
IGTM: www.igtm.co.uk
IMEX Frankfurt: www.imex-frankfurt.com
Insiderei: www.insiderei.com
Kitzbühel: www.kitzbuehel.com
Meraner Land: www.meranerland.com
Mountfalcon: www.mountfalcon.com
NMK: neuromarketing-wissen.de/neuromarketing-kongress/
PGAsE: www.pgae.com
Pur Südtirol: www.pursuedtirol.com
Red Rooster: www.redrooster.it
Roomkey: www.roomkey.com
Susanne Kaufmann: www.susannekaufmann.com
TechSmith: www.techsmith.com
theALPS: www.the-alps.eu
Tourism Meets Industry: www.tourism-meets-industry.com
World Travel Market: www.wtmlondon.com